W9-CCM-450

90 MINUTES IN HEAVEN

A TRUE STORY

of DEATH & LIFE

DON PIPER

WITH CECIL MURPHEY

Revell

a division of Baker Publishing Group
Grand Rapids, Michigan

© 2004, 2014, 2015 by Don Piper

Published by Revell
a division of Baker Publishing Group
P.O. Box 6287, Grand Rapids, MI 49516-6287
www.revellbooks.com

Paperback special edition published 2015

Printed in the United States of America

All rights reserved. No part of this publication may be reproduced, stored in a retrieval system, or transmitted in any form or by any means—for example, electronic, photocopy, recording—without the prior written permission of the publisher. The only exception is brief quotations in printed reviews.

Library of Congress Cataloging-in-Publication Data
Piper, Don, 1950-
90 minutes in heaven : a true story of death & life / Don Piper with Cecil Murphey Revell. — Special edition.
   pages cm
Includes bibliographical references.
ISBN 978-0-8007-2680-5 (pbk.)
1. Piper, Don, 1950– 2. Heaven—Christianity. 3. Near-death experiences—Religious aspects—Christianity. I. Murphey, Cecil. II. Title. III. Title: Ninety minutes in heaven.
BT846.3.P56 2015
231.7'3092—dc23   2015015415

Unless otherwise indicated, Scripture is taken from the *Holy Bible*, New Living Translation, copyright © 1996. Used by permission of Tyndale House Publishers, Inc., Wheaton, Illinois 60189. All rights reserved.

Scripture marked GW is taken from GOD'S WORD®. © 1995 God's Word to the Nations. Used by permission of Baker Publishing Group.

Scripture marked NIV is taken from the Holy Bible, New International Version®. NIV®. Copyright © 1973, 1978, 1984 by Biblica, Inc.™ Used by permission of Zondervan. All rights reserved worldwide. www.zondervan.com

Scripture marked KJV is taken from the King James Version of the Bible.

15   16   17   18   19   20   21   7   6   5   4   3   2   1

To the prayer warriors . . .
You prayed; I'm here

CONTENTS

PREFACE TO THE SPECIAL EDITION

The decade of the 1950s was a fascinating era to grow up in Europe. As the son of a career US Army soldier, I was a preschool child in France and Germany. Less than six years after Sgt. Ralph Piper invaded France with the Allied armada, Ralph, my mother Billie, and little Donnie were *residents' au Francais*. I marveled at the chateau that we shared with two other army families. There were cobblestoned streets, lovely gardens, and ivy-covered plaster walls enclosing the yard. Only years later did it occur to me that the holes in those walls were from World War II machine gun bullets fired only a few years before I was born in 1950.

For Americans living in Europe, life was very simple. Though the French seemed genuinely delighted that the Yanks were there, we were living in a cultural vacuum. Television had hardly begun to thrive stateside and was only a novelty in France. And then there was the language barrier. The street signs, the newspapers and magazines, the daily conversations of the natives...all in

French. As a child, the locals were not too hard on me for French mispronunciations. Foreign adults like my parents fared a little worse. Entertainment and fellowship for adult Americans consisted of dining together and playing canasta or hearts around a table, listening to 78 and 33 1/3 records, and taking in an occasional movie. Kids mostly did what kids do best: play.

It was while playing on the floor next to the card-dealing adults that I learned of something that would become a cherished part of my life; motion pictures. One night I overheard the adults talking about a new movie filmed in France, John Huston's *Moulin Rouge*. While our widowed landlord babysat us kids one night our parents went to the Paris premiere of this film. They didn't actually see the film; they stood outside in the Parisian night to see the movie stars Jose Ferrer and Zsa Zsa Gabor walk in to the movie's premiere. I was captivated by this talk of movies. As we continued to live in France and then moved to Germany, I heard them speak of films like *Shane, From Here to Eternity, Roman Holiday, Stalag 17, The Glen Miller Story, The Robe, On the Waterfront, Seven Brides for Seven Brothers, The Caine Mutiny, The High and the Mighty, White Christmas, Rebel Without a Cause, Guys and Dolls, The Seven Year Itch, Oklahoma, Giant, The King and I, Moby Dick*, and *High Society*. Listening in to the lonely Americans talk about movies, I became a movie buff.

Back in the United States the first movie I ever remember seeing was *The Wizard of Oz*. Its first television network broadcast was in 1956, and the yearly re-airing of it became a mainstay for a generation of American kids. I watched it with my new France-born brother Alan (named after movie star Alan Ladd) on a portable Admiral black and white TV set. Imagine my shock a few years later when I saw *The Wizard of OZ* again and discovered that Munchkin Land was actually in Technicolor! Produced in 1939, along with one of my other favorite films,

Gone With the Wind, it has dazzled millions. Over the years, other pictures have captured my heart; Zeffirelli's *Romeo and Juliet,* Spielberg's *Schindler's List* and *Saving Private Ryan,* movie musicals, slapstick comedies, and sports films. I love a good movie!

And now I am one!

Eleven years after my book was released and nearly twenty-seven years after the events of *90 Minutes in Heaven: A True Story of Death & Life* unfolded, the movie of the same name is completed. I must say that it is peculiar to be portrayed by another human being. Hayden Christensen, a fine young actor, is playing Don Piper, and Kate Bosworth, a winsome and accomplished actress, is portraying Eva Piper. Other cast members include Michael W. Smith, Fred Thompson, Michael Harding, Jason Kennedy, and Dwight Yoakum. Veteran Hollywood director Michael Polish skillfully helms this biopic.

It was my great privilege to be on set during principal photography. Happily, my entire immediate family was also able to be on set during the production. Eva, Nicole, Chris, and Joe got to meet the actors who portrayed them. *90 Minutes in Heaven* is one family's story of triumph over tragedy and purpose over pain. I do believe that you will be as highly inspired by this film as millions of readers have been inspired by this book.

It all began with the confidence of my co-writer and friend Cec Murphey, my editor Vicki Crumpton, and my publisher, Baker Publishing Group. This movie has its roots in the writing and publishing of this book. Along the way, my literary agent Deidre Knight and my theatrical agent, Sean Daily of Hotchkiss and Associates, fought for this project. I would like to thank the wonderful folks at Giving Films for getting behind this movie project, especially Giving Films CEO Rick Jackson. And many thanks to the Georgia Film Commission and the people of Greater Atlanta for their invaluable cooperation in making the film. Our cast and crew are ultimate professionals!

From a little boy who "traveled" to Oz and back with Dorothy in 1956 to the pastor who went to the gates of heaven and back in *90 Minutes in Heaven: The Movie,* it's been quite a journey. My first movie journey was a childhood fantasy. My accident and visit to heaven's gates…all too real.

A motion picture might not be worth a thousand words, but it goes a long way. My prayer is that you will enjoy the picture and the book that inspired it. After all, the goal of both is to help people get into heaven and have a better life on the way there.

I sign this book "see you at the gates." Perhaps for while at least it should change to "see you at the movies!" now that I am a movie. I hope to see you in both places.

Don Piper
April 2015

PUBLISHER'S PREFACE

In the summer of 2004 Baker Publishing Group released *90 Minutes in Heaven* with a modest first printing of 7500 copies. At the time, Don Piper was an unknown pastor with a bold claim. His book could have generated any type of reaction, including rejection or, more likely, indifference. Few people anticipated a bestseller, at least not openly.

Interest in Don's story developed slowly through word of mouth, until a tipping point arrived one year later. Bookstores sold out and reordered in larger quantities. The title appeared on major bestseller lists and began climbing. As interest grew for *90 Minutes in Heaven*, readers spoke of the impact of Don's story on their lives. They offered their own testimonies about pain, faith, and hope. It seemed that heaven was again on our minds.

From this process one lesson appeared swiftly: Don's experience was extraordinary, but it was not unique. Other people reported similar experiences, but these most recent stories were yet untold. At the time when *90 Minutes in Heaven* appeared, bookstores had not observed much current interest in afterlife stories, or much eagerness in readers for hearing and sharing those stories.

In the publishing offices, editors have been understandably hesitant about repeating fantastic reports. The reception of *90 Minutes in Heaven* led our profession to revisit that caution. In accepting the risk and responsibility for speaking out, Don Piper created a path for others. His rising profile generated a space—not merely for one book and one story, but for other amazing accounts of near-death experiences. These stories might have remained obscure had not *90 Minutes in Heaven* initiated a wide conversation, and the appearance of all these testimonies is thrilling to witness.

Reporting on near-heaven experiences in *Christianity Today*, editor Mark Galli wrote:

> One reason this writer is disposed to believe many of these stories, at least initially, is because they fit with what I as a historian have come to trust as real and true. I was asked a few years ago to moderate a panel in which Don *"90 Minutes in Heaven"* Piper was to participate. After speaking with him before and after the session, and hearing him explain his near-heaven experience during the panel, I was struck with this thought: *Piper is a reliable, trustworthy witness.* . . . As a Christian who believes there is more to this existence than the material, I do not dismiss out of hand the possibility of someone having an extraordinary heavenly experience. All manner of miracles have happened and continue to happen in our world. But a lot depends on the trustworthiness of the individual involved. And Piper simply had the look and sound of sanity, of someone who was telling the truth, whose word was his bond.[1]

A second lesson concerns hope. The popularity of Don's story reflects the urgency of hope, and that this hope comes from God and his promises. "Be not afraid," the Bible tells us over and over.

The promise of heavenly hope does not ignore the weight of our burdens here on earthly ground. Readers of *90 Minutes in*

Heaven have observed that Don describes his physical suffering as vividly as he does his heavenly encounter. This mingling of pain, joy, and hope mimics our own experiences and observations, and *90 Minutes in Heaven* would be easier to dismiss if not for this balance. An encouragement to "be not afraid" carries more influence when it comes from a person who has faced trauma as frightful as any human might experience. There is nothing flippant about Don's hope in heaven and in the injuries he endured to obtain that vision. This opportunity killed him. Literally.

Both celestial and messy, Don's testimony is widely accepted because it reflects the gospel promise for us today. At Lake Livingston, Texas, in January 1989, God performed a miracle. This story connects us to God's mysterious activity in our own lives and stories. It offers a promise of what is to come. As the publisher and a companion of Don Piper, participating in this conversation is our greatest privilege. We place this story in your hands as an invitation to hope.

Dwight Baker
President
Baker Publishing Group

A Personal Update
from Don Piper

The years slip by so briskly. It's been twenty-five years since my fatal accident on a lonely bridge on a cold, rainy, east Texas morning. Yet some days when the piercing pain revisits me, it seems as if that crash happened yesterday.

Fourteen years following those momentous events on the bridge, I released the chronicle of that ordeal in a book called *90 Minutes in Heaven: A True Story of Death & Life.*

The first sentence in the "Acknowledgments" section of that book's first edition is, "I wrote this book in self-defense."

I must say today as I write this update for this edition, I do so "in utter amazement!" rather than in self-defense. The enormous commercial and spiritual success of my book defies any sort of conventional wisdom. Many have said, and I agree, that the deeply emotional responses and subsequent phenomenal sales must be a "God thing." What other explanation makes any sense?

Consider that the book in its various forms has now sold over six million copies in forty-six languages! Since its release in

August 2004, it is one of the most successfully selling books in print in any language. And this from a book that initially had a first printing of 7500 copies! Prior to this edition, the paperback edition of *90 Minutes in Heaven* is in its eighty-second printing!

Indeed, what an awesome journey it has been since August 2004, when our church receptionist called my office and said, "Don, you have a package at the front desk."

The furthest thing from my mind as I passed by her desk later was that the package could be my first copy of *90 Minutes in Heaven*. Chills ran down my spine as I pulled my very own book out of its shipping envelope. Wow!

Since that auspicious day, I have . . .

Traveled just short of two million miles sharing the *90 Minutes in Heaven* testimony with over three thousand live audiences. A conservative estimate of the number of souls who have heard me speak in person is over one and a half million, from all over the world. I have personally autographed over a quarter of a million copies of *90 Minutes*.

The *90 Minutes in Heaven* story was shared in a tent in Husbondliden, Sweden; near the Artic Circle in Lapland, Finland; in the War Memorial Convention Hall in Lihue, Kauai; in Talkeetna, Alaska, in the shadow of Mt. Denali; on a ship off the coast of Malta; at Capital Baptist Church in Mexico City; in Moncton, New Brunswick; at a church in Paris, France; in San Juan, Puerto Rico; from the pulpit of First Baptist in Maryville, Illinois, where the pastor was murdered while preaching three weeks before; with the "Yoopers" in Marquette, Michigan; at a supper club in Leicester, England; in Bumpass, Virginia; on a fjord in Norway; in an Amish barn; in Bavaria; and in a town that actually bills itself as the "middle of nowhere," Ainsworth, Nebraska.

The great commission stipulates that we should take the gospel to the ends of the earth. While I haven't quite accomplished that daunting task, I have made a dent in it. Having preached in many countries and all fifty US states, I am very aware of how different we are and yet how much we are alike.

All this traveling has led me to stay in an incredible variety of accommodations: Over a thousand hotels (from five stars to minus-five stars), sleeping under everything from silk sheets to sheets with holes in them. Hyatts, Hiltons, Hamptons, Holiday Inns, La Quintas, Marriotts, Days Inns, Comfort Inns, and dozens of bed and breakfasts. I've also stayed in lodges, camps, dormitories, a hut called an *ubetjent* in Norway, an abandoned college, rental houses, and cars (yes, we've slept in cars). I have been honored to spend nights in private homes. My son Chris and I even spent the night at the guest quarters of a nunnery across from Mount St. Mary's University where I was a guest speaker. Yes, we ate breakfast with dozens of sisters in habits. For a few moments I actually felt like I was in an old Bing Crosby movie.

Therefore, you won't be surprised to know that I am a member of virtually every frequent flier, guest rewards, and rental car frequent rewards program in existence. All that really means is that I travel constantly. Besides flying every week, I have a Chevy Tahoe with 150,000 miles of speaking engagement trips on it—and it's my second car since I started sharing the *90 Minutes* story!

I've been in Opels, Mercedes, Isuzus, SEATs (a Spanish vehicle), Citroens, Fiats, Volvos—all of them rental cars. There have been minivans, SUVs, tiny sedans, trucks, taxis, and vehicles driven by volunteers sent to pick us up. Several times we've driven all night in order to be at a venue for a breakfast speaking engagement the next morning.

In the course of all these miles (and this is an astounding fact), I have never missed a scheduled ministry event, though we did have a couple of postponements due to inclement weather.

In the course of ministering in Jesus' name I have spoken in ancient cathedrals, church auditoriums, fellowship halls, historical churches, hysterical churches, civic centers, school auditoriums, shopping malls, banquet halls, a cornfield in South Dakota, campgrounds, open-air pavilions, an Amish barn, a bathroom (actually an underground dorm/shower/bathroom complex into which we were herded along with faculty and students during a tornado warning at Cedarville University in Ohio), assisted living centers, and tents both large and small.

There will be no denominations in heaven. I often say, "In heaven, nothing divides us." On earth I have spoken to congregations of Methodists, Episcopalians, Assemblies of God, Lutherans, Catholics, Baptists, Mennonites, Amish groups, Presbyterians, Wesleyans, Anglicans, African Methodist Episcopals, Reformed groups, Congregationalists, Brethren, Pentecostals, Nazarenes, Missionary Alliance groups, Church of God groups, Bible churches, Independents, charismatics, non-denominational groups, Messianic groups, and Evangelical Free groups.

It has been my honor to share with students at middle schools, high schools, and dozens of colleges and universities, both private and public.

I have been the keynote speaker at pastors' retreats, women's retreats, youth camps, and Christian conferences from Honolulu to Mackinac Island.

We've flown to the top of Alaska's twenty-thousand-foot Mt. Denali and spoken at fifty feet below sea level in El Centro, California.

Remarkably, we've heard our hosts excitedly say, "We've never had this many people come to our church (or event) before." Indeed, there have been incredible numbers of record crowds. There have been several occasions when more people were seated outside the main auditorium than inside, simply because they couldn't get in!

I told a couple of pastors over these years, "Don't look up at the ceiling. They may be lowering folks through the roof at any minute."

Hosts have distracted many fire marshals in order to complete an event. A pastor in Sweden exclaimed, "Dear Lord, no one has ever sat in our balcony before tonight!" A pastor in Illinois remarked after a particularly anointed event, "We haven't had this many folks in here since we had the mayor's funeral." Audiences from one hundred to one hundred thousand filed in, day in and day out. Our God is an awesome God.

Along the way, it has been my distinct privilege to share the platform with some of this era's finest spiritual leaders, including J. I. Packer, Donald Miller, Gary Chapman, Tony Campolo, Randy Alcorn, Francis Chan, Bill Wiese, Kathy Triccoli, Auntie Anne (Beiler), Philip Yancey, Jennifer O'Neill, William P. Young, David Meece, Barry McGuire, Phil Munsey, Pat Boone, and so many others.

I have spoken following such diverse special music as Native American drums, Hula dancers, and an Elvis impersonator in Las Vegas. I have heard the song "I Can Only Imagine," by MercyMe no less than one thousand times and "What a Friend We Have in Jesus," a million times. (Well, maybe only 999,000.)

From the beginning I vowed never to discriminate in response to speaking invitations. So, since the first book's release, I have shared with such utterly diverse groups as the Nebraska Concrete Paving Convention, the Communication Corporation, a Louisiana Oil Marketer's Convention, the Christian Legal Society of Hawaii, a Navajo Tribal Elder Meeting at the Sandia Resort Casino, the Rawhide Boys Ranch, a Sioux powwow at Ft. Peck Reservation, a Chiropractors convention, the NYC Learning Annex in Manhattan, a Real Estate Brokers meeting, the Disc Jockeys of America in Las Vegas, Kiwanis meetings, Lions meetings, mayors' prayer breakfasts, the governor of Iowa's prayer breakfast, college alumni meetings, the Billy Graham Chapel at the Louisiana State Penitentiary (Angola), the Halawa Correctional Facility in Hawaii, prisons all over Texas, juvenile correctional facilities, rehabilitation facilities, to terminally ill patients all over the country, a paralyzed football player, and dozens of Ilizarov patients.

Elaborate and simple introductions have preceded my ministry opportunities. From "here's the dead guy," to an introduction by Christian contemporary band Tenth Avenue North, who said, "Don Piper's coming out to speak. He's stinking awesome!"

Thousands of media interviews for TV, radio, magazines, and newspapers have interspersed ministry events. I am honored to have been interviewed by Bob Woodruff, Bill O'Reilly, Pat Robertson, Gordon Robertson, Sean Hannity, Morris Cerullo, Jan Crouch, Kerry Shook, Jim Burns, Paula White, Phil Munsey, D. James Kennedy, and Pat Boone, among many others. In addition to US media outlets, I've been invited to appear on God TV Europe, the BBC, Scottish TV, Australian TV, Swedish TV, Norwegian TV, Canadian TV, and 100 Huntley Street in Ontario.

At the onset of this response to *90 Minutes in Heaven*, I formed a 501 3C non-profit ministry. It's been my intention to use the revenue from book sales, offerings, and honoraria to benefit those who have little visible means of support. Sales of this book have benefited ministries all over the world. These profits have allowed me to go to Joplin, Missouri, after the horrific tornado, Louisiana after hurricane Isaac, Kentucky after an airliner crash, Virginia after the Virginia Tech murders, and dozens of other places suffering the aftermath of catastrophes and crises.

It's been a joy and privilege to raise many thousands of dollars in donations during fundraisers for schools, prisons, handicapped adults and children, senior adult living facilities, and many others. Thousands of books have been donated to prison ministries, libraries, churches, grief support groups, and military and hospital chaplains. *90 Minutes in Heaven* is now used as a teaching tool for hospital staffs, mortuaries, grief support workers, and first responders.

A seven-part DVD teaching series based on the book was recorded in Franklin, Tennessee, and has been used as curriculum for discipleship training from coast to coast.

One of my most vivid memories of my trip to heaven is the music. *90 Minutes in Heaven* has inspired several songs. Since its release I have received lyrics and music to numerous compositions inspired by my book. A complete album of songs about our story, called *Heaven Is Real*, was recorded by Nashville recording artists Nash 3.

My friend and coauthor, Cec Murphey, and I have written three more books together, and he has also coauthored a book with my wife, Eva. Our agent, Deidre Knight, is not just a consummate media professional but has become a dear friend to us all. Dr. Vicki Crumpton, the acquiring editor of *90 Minutes*, has guided this book every step of the way and shares much of the credit for its publication and content. My friends at Speak Up Speaker Services have seen to it that I haven't had a day off for eight years now. Well, not quite. Shirley Liechty and Carol and Gene Kent of SUSS are wonderful folks who not only schedule the vast majority of my speaking engagements but have become true friends as well.

This humble tome remains a testimony to the faith of Cec, our fearless agent Deidre, Vicki, and the other members of the awesome team at Baker Publishing Group's Revell division including publicist Suzanne Cross Burden, Twila Bennett, Karen Steele, Marilyn Gordon, and company president Dwight Baker.

This journey has not been solo. The Board of Directors of Don Piper Ministries has been indispensable, as we have sought to carry out the ministry's mission. The late chairman of the board, David Gentiles, and board members Rev. Cliff McArdle, Dr. Mark Forrest, Rev. Sonny Steed, and Eldon Pentecost have prayerfully paved the way for all our efforts. My son Chris has traveled at least a million of those travel miles with me. Scott Flenniken has helped in shipping and receiving and is director of our ministry efforts. And just as my wife, Eva, has been the hero of our story while we found our new normal, she has also supported my travel and outreach every step of the way.

Here are some of her observations about the events since the release of *90 Minutes*:

> As I've traveled with Don over the past nine years, there are two questions I'm almost always asked: "Are you *the wife*?" and "Do you ever get tired of hearing Don's testimony?"
>
> To the first I answer, "Yes, I am," which reminds me how lucky we are to still have Don with us. Watching the evidence of how God is using such a horrific experience to bring a message of hope to people around the world makes me proud to be "the wife."
>
> The answer to the second question is no. I never tire of hearing his story. More importantly I love watching the faces of people who are hearing it for the first time. It is an awesome and humbling experience. At the book table I've had the privilege of listening to those who share how much Don's story means to them, and how it gives them a sense of hope and encouragement. I've seen the smiles and the tears. I've felt the hugs.
>
> Through the ministry of *90 Minutes* I've met more of my Christian family, those with whom I will spend eternity. The book's success has presented its own set of challenges—frequent separations as Don travels, celebrating many holidays in different time zones, and living with a hallway full of book boxes.
>
> I continue to be amazed with the response. It just proves how God can take something horrific and use it for his glory. This "wife" is honored to be a part of that. No matter where Don is

in the world he will call every night at 10 o'clock. Even though he's not home, I know he's doing what he is called to do.

And my son Chris truly "fought the good fight and ran the good race" as he served with me on the firing line of faith. Here's his take on the *90 Minutes* phenomena:

It's quite strange to think that my father's accident would precipitate not one but two life-altering episodes for the Pipers. Understandably, the catastrophic physical injuries Dad sustained in the collision, and the emotional toll they took on him and all who cared for him, forever altered the dynamic of our family. If you're reading this book, you're likely familiar with the story described on television shows, on radio programs, in magazines, in newspapers, and documented at least a thousand times on YouTube.

Through much frustration, tenacity, patience, and prayer, all of us processed the accident in our own way and, as we humans tend to do, assimilated the lessons we learned into our everyday lives. When Dad mentioned that Revell decided to publish the book, we were very glad that more people would have an opportunity to hear the story. At the time, it was significant only because someone, or the several someones who made the decision to take on this project, thought this episode was worth recording and recounting.

When the book came out, and immediately began to garner attention from enthusiastic readers and media alike, we were excited that God had revealed a purpose in one of the more painful periods our family had endured. After Dad left his position at our home church to devote more time to giving his testimony, we began to notice a new energy in him that had been lost or hidden by years of physical pain and repressed emotional hurt. If you truly are as young as you feel, Dad was half his age.

There comes a time, however, when the enthusiasm over a new endeavor and the stresses associated with that endeavor intersect. Dad would come home from one of his two-hundred-plus events a year fulfilled and exhausted—processing the dozens of stories he'd heard from people who felt like he could understand their pain because of his own. You don't forget the faces of the people who tell you about a recently lost loved one, a terminal illness, physical abuse, chemical dependency, etc., when you try to sleep at night. I don't think Dad was doing much sleeping.

So when he asked me to assist him with running the ministry, I agreed to do so only after a lot of prayer and counsel. He was juggling more invitations than he could possibly answer along with making travel arrangements, shipping books, fielding appearance requests, and allocating funds from speaking and book sales to dozens of charities around the world.

I tried to keep up with him as he trekked around the world sharing the gospel through the lens of his testimony. I have endured long security lines, food poisoning because of late-night eats from questionable establishments, and harrowing routes through treacherous roadways because of faulty GPS devices. I have seen the incredible beauty of God's creation and the wonders of the world . . . half the time on the way to an airport. I have held the hands of people dying from cancer and fed homeless people shrimp cocktail and cheesecake under a bridge in Portland, Oregon.

I have seen hearts healed because they heard, in person, about the incredible grace bestowed on us by a loving God. I have been part of worship so moving that the windows of heaven opened and everything shimmered like gold. I have witnessed that holy moment when someone embraces Christ for the very first time.

I have yelled at my father with such intensity that the walls of our hotel room shook. I have hugged him with such sincerity that I felt like a little boy again. For six years, I devoted my life to this great purpose, one only a sovereign God could ordain.

Although I have recently taken a more limited role in my father's ministry, I am still so thankful for the time spent making sure he got to the right place at the right time and knowing what hotel to check into afterward. I suppose it could be said that Dad's accident defined my childhood, and this great journey over the last half-decade defined me as a man. I have been blessed and honored to play a part in the *90 Minutes* story as it unfolded and as it continues to unfold.

———

Never among our most ambitious hopes was the prospect that *90 Minutes in Heaven* would achieve the sort of amazing reach and impact that it has had. More books and millions of miles traveled to be in front of millions of people have followed. As astounding as those facts are, the real joy for me is the thousands of dollars we have been able to share with those in need worldwide. It's the visits that I've had with those recovering from tragedy and loss, especially those wearing external fixators. It's meeting people who I have prayed for on previous visits who are brought to meet me on subsequent visits. And the words, "See, we prayed and now they can walk on their own."

But above all, it's the thousands of souls I have seen come to Christ after reading the book or hearing the testimony. Men, women, boys, and girls who email me, call me, share with me at a book signing table or walk forward during an altar call to say, "I've just trusted the Lord as Savior!" Praise God!

In 2004, when I wrote my acknowledgments I penned words that ring even more true today: "Lord, I haven't always understood the whys of what happened, but I never stopped trusting you. I pray, Abba Father, that this humble effort to tell my story pleases you and blesses many. Amen."

I can say without reservation: my prayer has been answered! Just as the prayers of those who prayed for me that rainy day on the way to church were answered.

Predictably and poignantly, some of those whom I thanked in the preface to the first edition have now joined my welcoming committee in heaven; my father, Ralph Piper, my dear friend David Gentiles, and my mother-in-law, Ethel Pentecost. But I know where they are!

The Why Questions

The final chapter of *90 Minutes in Heaven* is entitled, "The Why Questions." Why did this happen to me? Was it because I was a skeptic about people who said they died and saw heaven and came back to tell about their experiences? I can now answer that question once and for all.

In these twenty-five years since my own experience, I have heard dozens of utterly sincere people share strikingly similar stories about their own deaths and heaven experiences. Exhilarating to me is the fact that not one of these individuals emerged from his or her experience without becoming a Christian, if they had not already been a Christ-follower! Conversely, I have had a few sincere souls relate (understandably) very privately that they had experienced a hellish torment at death. Again, whether they were believers in Christ before or not, they emerged from their respective traumas as true followers of Christ. Every one of them!

Perhaps one of the reasons that I had my death, visit to the gates of heaven, and grueling recovery trial is so that others could know that they were not alone in their experiences. I'm more than okay with that now. Not so much before that original book was released.

I asked, "Did God want me to know how real pain could feel so that I could understand the pain of others?" Ten years later I would answer unequivocally, "Yes!" Many thousands of people have told me so. I am absolutely humbled and deeply honored to do so. God knows that I looked for someone to understand and empathize when I wore the first femur external fixator and endured thirty-four surgeries and two years of rehabilitation. And God said to me, *you will become that person.* What a humbling privilege!

I also asked, "Did God want me to know how real heaven is?" Today I would say, "Without a doubt!" Since the book's release, how many hands of terminally ill folks have I held as I shared with them the reality and promise of heaven? How many invitations have I extended for people to make a reservation in heaven through Christ and Christ alone? How many funerals have I conducted since my own death, reminding mourners that to be absent from the body is to be present with the Lord for those who truly know him? I know heaven is real, and we're taking reservations today!

My final question in that first book was, "How can my experiences of death, heaven, and a long period of recovery benefit others?" First, I was knocked down, but not out. It is a question of learning to be not bitter, but better, and different.

Second, I live because of answered prayer. I had nothing to do with my coming back that day. Many thousands of prayers were launched on my behalf and God said yes! And here I am!

Third, only many miracles of God could have saved me that day and allowed me to walk as I now do. Shattered legs and a tattered arm are now restored. Brain damage and internal injuries vanished. God is still in the miracle business in the twenty-first century. I am living proof of that.

And finally, I stood there at the gates of heaven that day, more alive and complete than I have ever been here on earth. I was surrounded by those who had preceded me in death and who had helped me get to heaven by their words and actions. This remains the most real experience of my entire existence. Though I chose to keep it a sacred secret for a while, I now happily and without reservation shout, "Heaven is real and Jesus is the Way!"

I did ask a lot of questions at the end of the original book. On the occasion of my book's tenth anniversary I would say that the answer to all of them is Jesus, Jesus, and Jesus! He is the Way, the Truth, and the Life!

If this is your first time to read my simple book, I humbly ask that you consider Christ. Talking about overcoming, miracles, prayer, and heaven won't get you to heaven . . . only Jesus will.

It would be a distinct honor to meet each of you here on earth. But there are a lot of you and only one of me. So I say, that if I don't meet you here, I long to see you there

. . . at the gate!

Don Piper
April 2014

ACKNOWLEDGMENTS

I wrote this book in self-defense. In the years since 1989 I have seldom satisfied anyone with quick answers or brief encounters retelling my experiences. On radio, on TV, in newspapers, and from countless pulpits and other speaking engagements, I have generally left more unanswered questions than satisfactory responses. People consistently have wanted to know more . . . always more. I wrote three different manuscripts about this experience to satisfy inquiring minds. None of them satisfied me. That's when I prevailed upon one of America's distinguished authors to partner with me to write a book that would answer the most compelling issues concerning my death and life. Cecil Murphey, author of very successful biographies of such luminaries as Franklin Graham, Truett Cathey, B. J. Thomas, Dino Karsanakas, and Dr. Ben Carson, gave me the perspective I wanted to write the book I needed to write. You're holding it now.

Cec has become a devoted friend, confidant, and mentor. Indeed, one of the blessings of writing this book has been to know Cec Murphey. His passion for this project is felt on every page. Thank you, Cec! You are deeply appreciated. Likewise, the Knight Agency's Deidre Knight's belief in this project is much appreciated. And Dr. Vicki Crumpton of Baker Publishing Group is a person I have grown to admire. Her dedication to seeing this story in print is cherished.

I want to thank the staff of both Memorial Hermann Medical Center's Trauma Unit and St. Luke's Episcopal Hospital in Houston for their devotion to the healing arts. Special thanks to Dr. Thomas Greider, my orthopedic surgeon since that fateful night of January 18, 1989.

Precious people of God from many churches have allowed me to serve them. Not only were their prayers crucial to my survival but their presence has been a blessing to my ministry. Deep gratitude goes to South Park Baptist Church of Alvin, Texas, God's great prayer warriors. I would like to acknowledge the special contributions of First Baptist Church, Airline Baptist Church, and Barksdale Baptist Church, all of Bossier City, Louisiana. My father in the ministry, Dr. Damon V. Vaughn, former pastor of the first two of those churches is owed an immeasurable debt.

For standing faithfully with me in the days since my accident I express undying love for the First Baptist Church of Rosharon, Texas, along with Hunters' Glen Church and Murphy Road Baptist Church of Plano, Texas. Since 1996 I have called First Baptist Church of Pasadena, Texas, my place of service. Your support for this project has been sweet and unwavering. Thank you all for your patience, forbearance, prayers, and love.

To Anita Onerecker and her late husband, Dick, thank you for allowing God to use you so dramatically. To all my friends, brothers and sisters in Christ, who prayed so passionately, I thank you. Only God knows your sacrifices and kindnesses. Most of all, I thank my friends of many years, Cliff McArdle and David Gentiles, true gifts from God. Whether day or night, convenient or imposition, expedient or sacrificial, you have always been faithful. And thank you all for encouraging me to see this book to fruition.

Finally, I want to express profound gratitude to my wife's parents, Eldon and Ethel Pentecost, and my own parents, Ralph and Billie Piper, for their incalculable sacrifices and faithful support. To my three children, Nicole, Chris, and Joe, I say . . . God has given me children so much better than I could have ever deserved. I am highly blessed. How can I say thank you for all you have meant to me, even more so since that Wednesday so long ago? And to my wife of thirty years, Eva, no one should ever have had to do the things you've had to do for me. But you did them, faithfully, compassionately, and without hesitation. Of all my family and friends, only Eva comes closest to really knowing how painful this journey has been each day, for she has endured it with me. Eva, you are a gift from God.

Lord, you know I haven't always understood the whys of what has happened, but I've never stopped trusting you. I pray, Abba Father, that this humble effort to tell my story pleases you and blesses many. Amen.

Don Piper
February 2004

PROLOGUE

I died on January 18, 1989.

Paramedics reached the scene of the accident within minutes. They found no pulse and declared me dead. They covered me with a tarp so that onlookers wouldn't stare at me while they attended to the injuries of the others. I was completely unaware of the paramedics or anyone else around me.

Immediately after I died, I went straight to heaven.

While I was in heaven, a Baptist preacher came on the accident scene. Even though he knew I was dead, he rushed to my lifeless body and prayed for me. Despite the scoffing of the Emergency Medical Technicians (EMTs), he refused to stop praying.

At least ninety minutes after the EMTs pronounced me dead, God answered that man's prayers.

I returned to earth.

This is my story.

1

THE ACCIDENT

That is why we can say with confidence,
  "The Lord is my helper,
      so I will not be afraid.
    What can mere mortals do to me?"

Hebrews 13:6

The Baptist General Convention of Texas (BGCT) holds annual statewide conferences. In January 1989, they chose the north shore of Lake Livingston where the Union Baptist Association, composed of all Baptist churches in the greater Houston area, operates a large conference center called Trinity Pines. The conference focused on church growth, and I went because I was seriously considering starting a new church.

The conference started on Monday and was scheduled to end with lunch on Wednesday. On Tuesday night, I joined a BGCT executive and friend named J. V. Thomas for a long walk. J. V. had become a walker after his heart attack, so we exercised together the last night of the conference.

Months earlier, I had begun thinking that it was time for me to start a new congregation. Before embarking on such a venture, I wanted as much information as I could get. I knew that J. V. had as much experience and knowledge about new church development as anyone in the BGCT. Because he had started many successful churches in the state, most of us recognized him as the expert. As we walked together that night, we talked about my starting a new church, when to do it, and where to plant it. I wanted to know the hardships as well as the pitfalls to avoid. He answered my seemingly endless questions and raised issues I hadn't thought about.

We walked and talked for about an hour. Despite the cold, rainy weather, we had a wonderful time together. J. V. remembers that time well.

So do I, but for a different reason: It would be the last time I would ever walk normally.

On Wednesday morning the weather worsened. A steady rain fell. Had the temperature been only a few degrees colder, we couldn't have traveled, because everything would have been frozen.

The morning meetings started on time. The final speaker did something Baptist preachers almost never do—he finished early. Instead of lunch, the staff at Trinity Pines served us brunch at about ten thirty. I had packed the night before, so everything was stowed in my red 1986 Ford Escort.

As soon as we finished brunch, I said good-bye to all my friends and got into my car to drive back to the church where I was on staff, South Park Baptist Church in Alvin, a Houston bedroom community.

When I started the engine, I remembered that only three weeks earlier I had received a traffic ticket for not wearing a seat belt. I had been on my way to preach for a pastor friend who was going to have throat surgery. A Texas trooper had caught me. That ticket still lay on the passenger seat, reminding me to pay it as soon as I returned to Alvin. Until I received the ticket, I had not usually worn a seat belt, but after that I changed my ways.

When I looked at that ticket I thought, *I don't want to be stopped again.* So I carefully fastened my seat belt. That small act would be a crucial decision.

There were two ways to get back to Houston and on to Alvin. As soon as I reached the gates of Trinity Pines, I had to choose either to drive through Livingston and down Highway 59 or to head west to Huntsville and hit I-45, often called the Gulf Freeway. Each choice is probably about the same distance. Every other time to and from Trinity Pines I had driven Highway 59. That morning I decided to take the Gulf Freeway.

I was relieved that we had been able to leave early. It was only a few minutes after 11:00, so I could get back to the church by 2:00. The senior minister had led a group to the Holy Land and left me responsible for our midweek service at South Park Church. He had also asked me to preach for the next two Sundays. That night was a prayer meeting, which required little preparation, but I needed to work on my sermon for the following Sunday morning.

Before I left Alvin, I had written a draft for the first sermon titled "I Believe in a Great God." As I drove, I planned to glance over the sermon and evaluate what I had written so far.

Many times since then I've thought about my decision to take the Gulf Freeway. It's amazing how we pay no attention to simple decisions at the time they're made. Yet I would remind myself that even the smallest decisions often hold significant consequences. This was one of those choices.

I pulled out of Trinity Pines, turned right, and headed down Texas Highway 19. That would take me to Huntsville and intersect with I-45, leading to Houston. I didn't have to drive far before I reached Lake Livingston, a man-made lake, created by damming the Trinity River. What was once a riverbed is now a large, beautiful lake. Spanning Lake Livingston is a two-lane highway whose roadbed has been built up above the level of the lake. The road has no shoulders, making it extremely narrow. I would have to drive across a long expanse of water on that narrow road until I reached the other side. I had no premonitions about the trip, although I was aware of the road's lack of shoulders.

At the end of the highway across the lake is the original bridge over the Trinity River. Immediately after the bridge, the road rises sharply, climbing the bluff above the Trinity's riverbed. This sharp upturn makes visibility a problem for drivers in both directions.

This was my first time to see the bridge, and it looked curiously out of place. I have no idea of the span, but the bridge is quite long. It's an old bridge with a massive, rusty steel superstructure. Other than the immediate road ahead, I could see little, and I certainly didn't glimpse any other traffic. It was a dangerous bridge, and as I would learn later, several accidents had occurred on it. (Although no longer used, the bridge is still there. The state built another one beside it.)

I drove at about fifty miles an hour because it was, for me, uncharted territory. I braced my shoulders against the chill inside the car. The wind made the morning seem even colder than it was. The steady rain had turned into a cloudburst. I would be happy to finally reach Alvin again. About 11:45 a.m., just before I cleared the east end of the bridge, an eighteen-wheeler driven by an inmate, a trusty at the Texas Department of Corrections, weaved across the center line and hit my car head-on. The truck sandwiched my small car between the bridge railing and the driver's side of the truck. All those wheels went right on top of my car and smashed it.

I remember parts of the accident, but most of my information came from the accident report and people at the scene.

From the description I've received from witnesses, the truck then veered off to the other side of the narrow bridge and side-swiped two other cars. They were in front of the truck and had already passed me going in the opposite direction. The police record says that the truck was driving fast—at least sixty miles an hour—when it struck my car. The inexperienced driver finally brought the truck to a stop almost at the end of the bridge.

A young Vietnamese man was in one vehicle that was hit, and an elderly Caucasian man was in the other. Although shaken up, both drivers suffered only minor cuts and bruises. They refused help, so the paramedics transported neither man to the hospital.

Because of the truck's speed, the accident report states that the impact was about 110 miles an hour. That is, the truck struck me while going sixty miles an hour, and I was carefully cruising along at fifty. The inmate received a citation for failure to control his vehicle and speeding. Information later came out that the inmate wasn't licensed to drive the truck. At the prison, supervisors had asked for volunteers to drive their truck to pick up food items and bring them back. Because he was the only volunteer, they let him drive their supply truck. Two guards followed close behind him in another state-owned pickup.

After the accident, the truck driver didn't have a scratch on him. The prison truck received little damage. However, the heavy vehicle had crushed my Ford and pushed it from the narrow road. Only the bridge railing stopped my car from going into the lake.

According to those who were at the scene, the guards called for medical backup from the prison, and they arrived a few minutes later. Someone examined me, found no pulse, and declared that I had been killed instantly.

I have no recollection of the impact or anything that happened afterward.

In one powerful, overwhelming second, I died.

2
MY TIME IN HEAVEN

He was afraid and said, "How awesome is this place! This is none other than the house of God; this is the gate of heaven."

Genesis 28:17

When I died, I didn't flow through a long, dark tunnel. I had no sense of fading away or of coming back. I never felt my body being transported into the light. I heard no voices calling to me or anything else. Simultaneous with my last recollection of seeing the bridge and the rain, a light enveloped me, with a brilliance beyond earthly comprehension or description. Only that.

In my next moment of awareness, I was standing in heaven.

Joy pulsated through me as I looked around, and at that moment I became aware of a large crowd of people. They stood in front of a brilliant, ornate gate. I have no idea how far away they were; such things as distance didn't matter. As the crowd rushed toward me, I didn't see Jesus, but I did see people I had known. As they surged toward me, I knew instantly that all of them had died during my lifetime. Their presence seemed absolutely natural.

They rushed toward me, and every person was smiling, shouting, and praising God. Although no one said so, intuitively I knew they were my celestial welcoming committee. It was as if they had all gathered just outside heaven's gate, waiting for me.

The first person I recognized was Joe Kulbeth, my grandfather. He looked exactly as I remembered him, with his shock of white hair and what I called a big banana nose. He stopped momentarily and stood in front of me. A grin covered his face. I may have called his name, but I'm not sure.

"Donnie!" (That's what my grandfather always called me.) His eyes lit up, and he held out his arms as he took the last steps toward me. He embraced me, holding me tightly. He was once again the robust, strong grandfather I had remembered as a child.

I'd been with him when he suffered a heart attack at home and had ridden with him in the ambulance. I had been standing just outside the emergency room at the hospital when the doctor walked out and faced me. He shook his head and said softly, "We did everything we could."

My grandfather released me, and as I stared into his face, an ecstatic bliss overwhelmed me. I didn't think about his heart attack or his death, because I couldn't get past the joy of our reunion. How either of us reached heaven seemed irrelevant.

I have no idea why my grandfather was the first person I saw. Perhaps it had something to do with my being there when he died. He wasn't one of the great spiritual guides of my life, although he certainly influenced me positively in that way.

After being hugged by my grandfather, I don't remember who was second or third. The crowd surrounded me. Some hugged me and a few kissed my cheek, while others pumped my hand. Never had I felt more loved.

One person in that greeting committee was Mike Wood, my childhood friend. Mike was special because he invited me to Sunday school and was influential in my becoming a Christian. Mike was the most devoted young Christian I knew. He was also a popular kid and had lettered four years in football, basketball, and track and field, an amazing feat. He also became a hero to me, because he lived the Christian lifestyle he often talked about. After high school, Mike received a full scholarship to Louisiana State University. When he was nineteen, Mike was killed in a car wreck. It broke my heart when I heard about his death, and it took me a long time to get over it. His death was the biggest shock and most painful experience I'd had up to that time in my life.

When I attended his funeral, I wondered if I would ever stop crying. I couldn't understand why God had taken such a dedicated disciple. Through the years since then, I had never been able to forget the pain and sense of loss. Not that I thought of him all the time, but when I did, sadness came over me.

Now I saw Mike in heaven. As he slipped his arm around my shoulder, my pain and grief vanished. Never had I seen Mike smile so brightly. I still didn't know why, but the joyousness of the place wiped away any questions. Everything felt blissful. Perfect.

More and more people reached for me and called me by name. I felt overwhelmed by the number of people who had come to welcome me to heaven. There were so many of them, and I had never imagined anyone being as happy as they all were. Their faces radiated a serenity I had never seen on earth. All were full of life and expressed radiant joy.

Time had no meaning. However, for clarity, I'll relate this experience in terms that refer to time.

I saw my great-grandfather, heard his voice, and felt his embrace as he told me how excited he was that I had come to join them. I saw Barry Wilson, who had been my classmate in high school but later drowned in a lake. Barry hugged me, and his smile radiated a happiness I didn't know was possible. He and everyone that followed praised God and told me how excited they were to see me and to welcome me to heaven and to the fellowship they enjoyed.

Just then, I spotted two teachers who had loved me and often talked to me about Jesus Christ. As I walked among them, I became aware of the wide variety of ages—old and young and every age in-between. Many of them hadn't known each other on earth, but each had influenced my life in some way. Even though they hadn't met on earth, they seemed to know each other now.

As I try to explain this, my words seem weak and hardly adequate, because I have to use earthly terms to refer to unimaginable joy, excitement, warmth, and total happiness. Everyone continually embraced me, touched me, spoke to me, laughed, and praised God. This seemed to go on for a long time, but I didn't tire of it.

My father is one of eleven children. Some of his brothers and sisters had as many as thirteen children. When I was a kid, our family reunions were so huge we rented an entire city park in Monticello, Arkansas. We Pipers are affectionate, with a lot of hugging and kissing whenever we come together. None of those earthly family reunions, however, prepared me for the sublime gathering of saints I experienced at the gates of heaven.

Those who had gathered at Monticello were some of the same people waiting for me at the gates of heaven. Heaven was many things, but without a doubt, it was the greatest family reunion of all.

Everything I experienced was like a first-class buffet for the senses. I had never felt such powerful embraces or feasted my eyes on such beauty. Heaven's light and texture defy earthly eyes or explanation. Warm, radiant light engulfed me. As I looked around, I could hardly grasp the vivid, dazzling colors. Every hue and tone surpassed anything I had ever seen.

With all the heightened awareness of my senses, I felt as if I had never seen, heard, or felt anything so real before. I don't recall that I tasted anything, yet I knew that if I had, that too would have been more glorious than anything I had eaten or drunk on earth. The best way I can explain it is to say that I felt as if I were in another dimension. Never, even in my happiest moments, had I ever felt so fully alive. I stood speechless in front of the crowd of loved ones, still trying to take in everything. Over and over I heard how overjoyed they were to see me and how excited they were to have me among them. I'm not sure if they actually said the words or not, but I knew they had been waiting and expecting me, yet I also knew that in heaven there is no sense of time passing.

I gazed at all the faces again as I realized that they all had contributed to my becoming a Christian or had encouraged me in my growth as a believer. Each one had affected me positively. Each had spiritually impacted me in some way and helped make me a better disciple. I knew—again one of those things I knew without being aware of how I had absorbed that information—that because of their influence I was able to be present with them in heaven.

We didn't talk about what they had done for me. Our conversations centered on the joy of my being there and how happy they were to see me.

Still overwhelmed, I didn't know how to respond to their welcoming words. "I'm happy to be with you," I said, and even those words couldn't express the utter joy of being surrounded and embraced by all those people I loved.

I wasn't conscious of anything I'd left behind and felt no regrets about leaving family or possessions. It was as if God had removed anything negative or worrisome from my consciousness, and I could only rejoice at being together with these wonderful people.

They looked exactly as I once knew them—although they were more radiant and joyful than they'd ever been on earth.

My great-grandmother, Hattie Mann, was Native American. As a child I saw her only after she had developed osteoporosis. Her head and shoulders were bent forward, giving her a humped appearance. I especially remember her extremely wrinkled face. The other thing that stands out in my memory is that she had false teeth—which she didn't wear often. Yet when she smiled at me in heaven, her teeth sparkled. I knew they were her own, and when she smiled, it was the most beautiful smile I had ever seen.

Then I noticed something else—she wasn't slumped over. She stood strong and upright, and the wrinkles had been erased from her face. I have no idea what age she was, and I didn't even think about that. As I stared at her beaming face, I sensed that age has no meaning in heaven.

Age expresses time passing, and there is no time there. All of the people I encountered were the same age they had been the last time I had seen them—except that all the ravages of living on earth had vanished. Even though some of their features may not have been considered attractive on earth, in heaven every feature was perfect, beautiful, and wonderful to gaze at.

Even now, years later, I can sometimes close my eyes and see those perfect countenances and smiles that surprised me with the most human warmth and friendliness I've ever witnessed. Just being with them was a holy moment and remains a treasured hope.

When I first stood in heaven, they were still in front of me and came rushing toward me. They embraced me, and no matter which direction I looked, I saw someone I had loved and who had loved me. They surrounded me, moving around so that everyone had a chance to welcome me to heaven.

I felt loved—more loved than ever before in my life. They didn't say they loved me. I don't remember what words they spoke. When they gazed at me, I *knew* what the Bible means by perfect love. It emanated from every person who surrounded me.

I stared at them, and as I did I felt as if I absorbed their love for me. At some point, I looked around and the sight overwhelmed me. Everything was brilliantly intense. Coming out from the gate—a short distance ahead—was a brilliance that was brighter than the light that surrounded us, utterly luminous. As soon as I stopped gazing at the people's faces, I realized that everything around me glowed with a dazzling intensity. In trying to describe the scene, words are totally inadequate, because human words can't express the feelings of awe and wonder at what I beheld.

Everything I saw glowed with intense brightness. The best I can describe it is that we began to move toward that light. No one said it was time to do so, and yet we all started forward at the same time. As I stared ahead, everything seemed to grow taller—like a gentle hill that kept going upward and never stopped. I had expected to see some darkness behind the gate, but as far ahead as I could see, there was absolutely nothing but intense, radiant light.

By contrast, the powerful light I had encountered when I met my friends and loved ones paled into darkness as the radiance and iridescence in front of me increased. It was as if each step I took intensified the glowing luminosity. I didn't know how it could get more dazzling, but it did. It would be like cracking open the door of a dark room and walking into the brightness of a noonday sun. As the door swings open, the full rays of the sun burst forth, and we're momentarily blinded.

I wasn't blinded, but I was amazed that the luster and intensity continually increased. Strange as it seems, as brilliant as everything was, each time I stepped forward, the splendor increased. The farther I walked, the brighter the light. The light engulfed me, and I had the sense that I was being ushered into the presence of God. Although our earthly eyes must gradually adjust to light or darkness, my heavenly eyes saw with absolute ease. In heaven, each of our senses is immeasurably heightened to take it all in. And what a sensory celebration!

A holy awe came over me as I stepped forward. I had no idea what lay ahead, but I sensed that with each step I took, it would grow more wondrous.

Then I heard the music.

3

HEAVENLY MUSIC

Then I looked again, and I heard the singing of thousands and millions of angels around the throne and the living beings and the elders.

Revelation 5:11

As a young boy I spent a lot of time out in the country and woods. When walking through waist-high dried grass, I often surprised a covey of birds and flushed them out of their nests on the ground. A whooshing sound accompanied their wings as they flew away.

My most vivid memory of heaven is what I heard. I can only describe it as a holy swoosh of wings.

But I'd have to magnify that thousands of times to explain the effect of the sound in heaven.

It was the most beautiful and pleasant sound I've ever heard, and it didn't stop. It was like a song that goes on forever. I felt awestruck, wanting only to listen. I didn't just hear music. It seemed as if I were part of the music—and it played in and through my body. I stood still, and yet I felt embraced by the sounds.

As aware as I became of the joyous sounds and melodies that filled the air, I wasn't distracted. I felt as if the heavenly concert permeated every part of my being, and at the same time I focused on everything else around me.

I never saw anything that produced the sound. I had the sense that whatever made the heavenly music was just above me, but I didn't look up. I'm not sure why. Perhaps it was because I was so enamored with the people around me, or maybe it was because my senses were so engaged that I feasted on everything at the same time. I asked no questions and never wondered about anything. Everything was perfect. I sensed that I knew everything and had no questions to ask.

Myriads of sounds so filled my mind and heart that it's difficult to explain them. The most amazing one, however, was the angels' wings. I didn't see them, but the sound was a beautiful, holy melody with a cadence that seemed never to stop. The swishing resounded as if it was a form of never-ending praise. As I listened I simply *knew* what it was.

A second sound remains, even today, the single, most vivid memory I have of my entire heavenly experience. I call it music, but it differed from anything I had ever heard or ever expect to hear on the earth. The melodies of praise filled the atmosphere. The nonstop intensity and endless variety overwhelmed me.

The praise was unending, but the most remarkable thing to me was that hundreds of songs were being sung at the same time—all of them worshiping God. As I approached the large, magnificent gate, I heard them from every direction and realized that each voice praised God. I write *voice*, but it was more than that. Some sounded instrumental, but I wasn't sure—and I wasn't concerned. Praise was everywhere, and all of it was musical, yet comprised of melodies and tones I'd never experienced before.

"Hallelujah!" "Praise!" "Glory to God!" "Praise to the King!" Such words rang out in the midst of all the music. I don't know if angels were singing them or if they came from humans. I felt so awestruck and caught up in the heavenly mood that I didn't look around. My heart filled with the deepest joy I've ever experienced. I wasn't a participant in the worship, yet I felt as if my heart rang out with the same kind of joy and exuberance.

If we played three CDs of praise at the same time, we'd have a cacophony of noise that would drive us crazy. This was totally different. Every sound blended, and each voice or instrument enhanced the others.

As strange as it may seem, I could clearly distinguish each song. It sounded as if each hymn of praise was meant for me to hear as I moved toward the gates.

Many of the old hymns and choruses I had sung at various times in my life were part of the music—along with hundreds of songs I had never heard before. Hymns of praise, modern-sounding choruses, and ancient chants filled my ears and brought not only a deep peace but the greatest feeling of joy I've ever experienced.

As I stood before the gate, I didn't think of it, but later I realized that I didn't hear such songs as "The Old Rugged Cross" or "The Nail-Scarred Hand." None of the hymns that filled the air were about Jesus' sacrifice or death. I heard no sad songs and instinctively knew that there are no sad songs in heaven. Why would there be? All were praises about Christ's reign as King of Kings and our joyful worship for all he has done for us and how wonderful he is.

The celestial tunes surpassed any I had ever heard. I couldn't calculate the number of songs—perhaps thousands—offered up simultaneously, and yet there was no chaos, because I had the capacity to hear each one and discern the lyrics and melody.

I marveled at the glorious music. Though not possessed of a great singing voice in life, I knew that if I sang, my voice would be in perfect pitch and would sound as melodious and harmonious as the thousands of other voices and instruments that filled my ears.

Even now, back on earth, sometimes I still hear faint echoes of that music. When I'm especially tired and lie in bed with my eyes closed, occasionally I drift off to sleep with the sounds of heaven filling my heart and mind. No matter how difficult a day I've had, peace immediately fills every part of my being. I still have flashbacks, although they're different from what we normally refer to as flashbacks. Mine are more flashbacks of the sounds than the sights.

As I've pondered the meaning of the memory of the music, it seems curious. I would have expected the most memorable experience to be something I had seen or the physical embrace of a loved one. Yet above everything else, I cherish those sounds, and at times I think, *I can't wait to hear them again—in person.* It's what I look forward to. I want to see everybody, but I know I'll be with them forever. I want to experience everything heaven offers, but most of all, I want to hear those never-ending songs again.

Obviously, I can't really know how God feels, but I find joy and comfort in thinking that he must be pleased and blessed by the continuous sounds of praise.

⁓

In those minutes—and they held no sense of time for me—others touched me, and their warm embraces were absolutely real. I saw colors I would never have believed existed. I've never, ever felt more alive than I did then.

I was home; I was where I belonged. I wanted to be there more than I had ever wanted to be anywhere on earth. Time had slipped away, and I was simply present in heaven. All worries, anxieties, and concerns vanished. I had no needs, and I felt perfect.

⁓

I get frustrated describing what heaven was like, because I can't begin to put into words what it looked like, sounded like, and felt like. It was perfect, and I knew I had no needs and never would again. I didn't even think of earth or those left behind.

I did not see God. Although I knew God was there, I never saw any kind of image or luminous glow to indicate his divine presence. I've heard people talk about going inside and coming back out the gate. That didn't happen to me.

I saw only a bright iridescence. I peered through the gate, yearning to see what lay beyond. It wasn't an anxious yearning, but a peaceful openness to experience all the grace and joy of heaven.

The only way I've made sense out of that part of the experience is to think that if I had actually seen God, I would never have wanted to return. My feeling has been that once we're actually in God's presence, we will never return to earth again, because it will be empty and meaningless by comparison.

For me, just to reach the gates was amazing. It was a foretaste of joy divine. My words are too feeble to describe what took place.

As a pastor, I've stood at the foot of many caskets and done many funerals and said, "To be absent from the body is to be present with the Lord to those who love him and know him."

I believed those words before. I believe them even more now.

⚊

After a time (I'm resorting to human terms again), we started moving together right up to the gate. No one said it, but I simply knew God had sent all those people to escort me inside the portals of heaven.

Looming just over the heads of my reception committee stood an awesome gate interrupting a wall that faded out of sight in both directions. It struck me that the actual entrance was small in comparison to the massive gate itself. I stared, but I couldn't see the end of the walls in either direction. As I gazed upward, I couldn't see the top either.

One thing did surprise me: On earth, whenever I thought of heaven, I anticipated that one day I'd see a gate made of pearls, because the Bible refers to the gates of pearl. The gate wasn't made of pearls, but was pearlescent—perhaps *iridescent* may be more descriptive. To me, it looked as if someone had spread pearl icing on a cake. The gate glowed and shimmered.

I paused and stared at the glorious hues and shimmering shades. The luminescence dazzled me, and I would have been content to stay at that spot. Yet I stepped forward as if being escorted into God's presence.

I paused just outside the gate, and I could see inside. It was like a city with paved streets. To my amazement, they had been constructed of literal gold. If you imagine a street paved with gold bricks, that's as close as I can come to describing what lay inside the gate.

Everything I saw was bright—the brightest colors my eyes had ever beheld—so powerful that no earthly human could take in this brilliance.

In the midst of that powerful scene, I continued to step closer to the gate and assumed that I would go inside. My friends and relatives were all in front of me, calling, urging, and inviting me to follow.

Then the scene changed. I can explain it only by saying that instead of their being in front of me, they were beside me. I felt that they wanted to walk beside me as I passed through the iridescent gate.

Sometimes people have asked me, "How did you move? Did you walk? Did you float?" I don't know. I just moved along with that welcoming crowd. As we came closer to the gate, the music increased and became even more vivid. It would be like walking up to a glorious event after hearing the faint sounds and seeing everything from a distance. The closer we got, the more intense, alive, and vivid everything became. Just as I reached the gate, my senses were even more heightened, and I felt deliriously happy.

I paused—I'm not sure why—just outside the gate. I was thrilled at the prospect and wanted to go inside. I knew everything would be even more thrilling than what I had experienced so far. At that very moment I was about to realize the yearning of every human heart. I was in heaven and ready to go in through the pearlescent gate.

During that momentary pause, something else changed. Instead of just hearing the music and the thousands of voices praising God, I had become part of the choir. I was one with them, and they had absorbed me into their midst. I had arrived at a place I had wanted to visit for a long time; I lingered to gaze before I continued forward.

Then, just as suddenly as I had arrived at the gates of heaven, I left them.

4

FROM HEAVEN TO EARTH

Even when I walk
    through the dark valley of death,
I will not be afraid,
    for you are close beside me.
Your rod and your staff
    protect and comfort me.

Psalm 23:4

The EMTs pronounced me dead as soon as they arrived at the scene. They stated that I died instantly. According to the report, the collision occurred at 11:45 a.m. The EMTs became so busy working with the others involved, that it was about 1:15 p.m. before they were ready to move me. They checked for a pulse once again.

I was still dead.

The state law said they had to pronounce me dead officially before they could remove my body from the scene of the accident. Unless they declared me dead, an ambulance would have to transport my body to a hospital. That county didn't have a coroner, but I learned later that a justice of the peace could declare me dead, and then they could remove my body.

Ambulances had come from the prison, the county, and Huntsville. Except for one, all of them left without taking back any patients. The last one was preparing to leave. From information I've pieced together, someone had arranged for an unmarked vehicle to take my body to a mortuary.

They had called for the Jaws of Life[1] to get me out of the smashed car. Because I was dead, there seemed to be no need for speed. Their concern focused on clearing the bridge for traffic to flow again.

When the truck came in at an angle and went right over the top of me, the truck smashed the car's ceiling, and the dashboard came down across my legs, crushing my right leg. My left leg was shattered in two places between the car seat and the dashboard. My left arm went over the top of my head, was dislocated, and swung backward over the seat. It was still attached—barely.

That left arm had been lying on the driver's side door, because I had been driving with my right hand. As I would learn later, the major bones were now missing, so my lower left arm was just a piece of flesh that held the hand to the rest of the arm. It was the same with the left leg. There was some tissue just above my knee that still fed blood to the calf and foot below. Four and a half inches of femur were missing and never found. The doctors have no medical explanation why I didn't lose all the blood in my body.

Glass and blood had sprayed everywhere. I had all kinds of small holes in my face from embedded glass. The steering wheel had pounded into my chest. Blood seeped out of my eyes, ears, and nose.

Just from seeing the results of the crash, the EMTs knew I had to have sustained massive head injuries and that my insides were completely rearranged. When he first felt no pulse, one of the EMTs covered me with a waterproof tarp that also blocked off the top of the car. They made no attempt to move me or try to get me out immediately—they couldn't have anyway, because it would have been impossible for them to drag or lift me out of the vehicle without the Jaws of Life.

One thing that sped help to the scene was that the two prison guards in the pickup truck immediately called for emergency assistance from the prison. Otherwise, we would have been too far away for any emergency vehicle to get to us quickly.

They examined the drivers of the other two cars; both of them were uninjured and refused medical attention. The prisoner who drove the truck sustained no injuries. As soon as the EMTs determined he was all right, they transported him back to the prison. Police halted all traffic on the bridge and waited for the ambulance to arrive. While they waited, traffic backed up for miles in both directions, especially the direction I had come from. It was only a narrow two-lane bridge, not wide enough for a car to turn around. Even if the waiting traffic could have turned around, they would have had to drive an extra forty or fifty miles around the lake to reach another road leading to their destination.

From the backed-up traffic, Dick and Anita Onerecker walked at least half a mile to the scene of the accident. Dick and Anita had started a church in Klein, which is north of Houston. Both had spoken at the conference I'd just attended. I'm not positive we actually met at Trinity Pines, although we may have. For years I had heard of Dick Onerecker, but that conference was the first time I had ever seen him.

On Wednesday morning, the Onereckers left Trinity Pines a few minutes before I did. By Houston standards, that January morning was extremely cold. As they sped along, Anita said, "I'm really chilled. Could we stop for coffee? I think that would warm me up."

Dick spotted a bait shop right on Lake Livingston, so they pulled over. Apparently, while they were buying coffee, I drove past them.

Many times afterward, Dick would bury his face in his hands and say, "You know that could easily have been us. It should have been us, but because we stopped and you drove past us, you got hit."

Before the Onereckers reached the bridge, the accident had occurred and traffic had started to back up. People got out of their cars and milled around, asking questions and sharing their limited information.

After Dick and Anita got out of their car, they asked fellow drivers, "What's going on up there?"

The word had passed down that there had been a serious auto accident. "A truck crashed into a car" was about all anyone knew.

Dick and Anita stood around a few minutes, but nothing happened, and more cars lined up behind them. Sometime between 12:30 and 12:45, they decided to walk to the accident site. When they saw a police officer, Dick said, "I'm a minister. Is there anybody here I can help? Is there anyone I can pray for?"

The police officer shook his head. "The people in those two cars," he said and pointed, "are shaken up a little bit but they're fine. Talk to them if you'd like."

"What about the other vehicle? The one with the tarp over it?"

"The man in the red car is deceased."

While Dick talked to the officer, Anita went over to the other vehicles. She gave her barely touched coffee to the old man.

Dick would later tell it this way: "God spoke to me and said, 'You need to pray for the man in the red car.'" Dick was an outstanding Baptist preacher. Praying for a dead man certainly ran counter to his theology. *I can't do that*, he thought. *How can I go over there and pray? The man is dead.*

The rain had become a light drizzle, but Dick was oblivious to his surroundings. Dick stared at the officer, knowing that what he would say wouldn't make sense. Yet God spoke to him so clearly that he had no doubt about what he was to do. God had told him to pray for a dead man. As bizarre as that seemed to him, Dick also had no doubt that the Holy Spirit was prompting him to act.

"I'd like to pray for the man in the red car," Dick finally said to the officer.

"Like I said, he's dead."

"I know this sounds strange, but I want to pray for him anyway."

The officer stared at him a long time before he finally said, "Well, you know, if that's what you want to do, go ahead, but I've got to tell you it's an awful sight. He's dead, and it's really a mess under the tarp. Blood and glass are everywhere, and the body's all mangled."

Dick, then in his forties, said, "I was a medic in Vietnam, so the idea of blood doesn't bother me."

"I have to warn you—" The man stopped, shrugged, and said, "Do what you want, but I'll tell you that you haven't seen anybody this bad."

"Thanks," Dick said and walked to the tarp-covered car.

From the pictures of that smashed-down car, it's almost impossible to believe, but somehow Dick actually crawled into the trunk of my Ford. It had been a hatchback, but that part of the car had been severed. I was still covered by the tarp, which he didn't remove, so it was extremely dark inside the car. Dick crept in behind me, leaned over the backseat, and put his hand on my right shoulder.

He began praying for me. As he said later, "I felt compelled to pray. I didn't know who the man was or whether he was a believer. I knew only that God told me I had to pray for him."

As Dick prayed, he became quite emotional and broke down and cried several times. Then he sang. Dick had an excellent voice and often sang publicly. He paused several times to sing a hymn and then went back to prayer.

Not only did Dick believe God had called him to pray for me but he prayed quite specifically that I would be delivered from unseen injuries, meaning brain and internal injuries.

This sounds strange, because Dick knew I was dead. Not only had the police officer told him but he also had checked for a pulse. He had no idea why he prayed as he did, except God told him to. He didn't pray for the injuries he could see, only for the healing of internal damage. He said he prayed the most passionate, fervent, emotional prayer of his life. As I would later learn, Dick was a highly emotional man anyway.

Then he began to sing again. "O what peace we often forfeit, O what needless pain we bear, all because we do not carry everything to God in prayer!"[2] The only thing I personally know for certain about the entire event is that as he sang the blessed old hymn "What a Friend We Have in Jesus," I began to sing with him.

In that first moment of consciousness, I was aware of two things. First, I was singing—a different kind of singing than the tones of heaven—I heard my own voice and then became aware of someone else singing.

The second thing I was aware of was that someone clutched my hand. It was a strong, powerful touch and the first physical sensation I experienced with my return to earthly life.

More than a year would lapse before I understood the significance of that hand clasping mine.

5

Earth to Hospital

But they were looking for a better place, a heavenly homeland.
That is why God is not ashamed to be called their God, for he
has prepared a heavenly city for them.

Hebrews 11:16

I'm not certain what the world record is for exiting a wrecked
car, but Dick Onerecker must have surely broken it that
Wednesday afternoon. When a dead man began to sing with
him, Dick scrambled out of that smashed car and raced over
to the nearest EMT.

"The man's alive! He's not dead! He's alive!"

Who would have believed him? A preacher had started to
pray for a man who had been dead for an hour and a half. Then
he dashed across the road shouting, "That man has come back
to life!"

The EMT stared.

"He's alive! The dead man started singing with me."

The words didn't make sense as Dick thought of them later,
but he could only keep yelling, "He's singing! He's alive!"

"Oh really?" a paramedic asked.

"I'm serious, this man's alive."

"We're medical professionals. We know a dead guy when we see him. That guy is *dead*."

"I'm telling you, that man just sang with me. He's alive."

"The justice of the peace is on his way here." He explained that although they knew I was dead, they couldn't move my body until someone in authority actually declared me dead. "But I can tell you this much: He is dead." The man turned away from Dick and refused to go over to my car.

Several ambulances had already arrived and departed.

Dick walked up in front of the remaining ambulance and said to the driver, "That man is alive. Go look at him."

The EMT began to act as if he handled feebleminded people all the time. "Please, we know our business. That man is—"

"Listen to me! I'm going to lie down on this bridge, and if you don't come over here, you're going to have to run over me."

"He's dead."

"Then humor me. Just feel his pulse," Dick pleaded.

"Okay, we'll check on him for you," the man said, mumbling under his breath. He walked over to the car, raised the tarp, reached inside, and found my right arm. He felt my pulse.

Everyone leaped into action. They began trying to figure out how to get me out. They could have taken me out on one side, but it would have been without my left leg. There was no clearance from the dashboard between my left leg and the seat, so they would have had to amputate. My leg was barely hanging on to my body anyway. I'm not sure they could have gotten my right leg out either. The point is that even though they could have gotten me out without the equipment, they would have left some of me in the car. They decided to wait on the proper equipment. They got on the phone and ordered the Jaws of Life to hurry from Huntsville, which was at least thirty miles away. I'm sure they did whatever they could for me, but I remember nothing. I remained vaguely conscious of people moving around me, touching me, and talking. I heard voices, but I couldn't make sense of anything they said. Dick refused to leave me. He got back inside the car, where he was able to kneel behind me, and he continued to pray until the Jaws of Life arrived. Only after they lifted me into the ambulance did he leave my side. When the EMTs lifted me out of the car, I remember that it involved a number of men—at least six or seven. As they moved me, I heard them talking about my leg. One of them said something about being careful so that my left leg didn't come off.

My system was in shock, so I felt no pain—not then, anyway. That came later.

They laid me on a gurney and started to roll me toward the ambulance. A light mist sprayed my face, and I saw nothing except the superstructure of the bridge above me. I was unable to move my head. I heard people walking around and glass crunching under their feet. They kept their voices low, so I had trouble following what they were saying.

I remember thinking, *Something terrible has happened here, and I think it's happened to me.* Even when I knew they were moving me into the ambulance, I felt weightless.

I don't remember anything about the ambulance ride, but later I learned that we went to two hospitals, both of which were little more than rural clinics.

"There's nothing we can do for him," I heard one doctor say as he examined me. "He's not going to make it. You may have gotten him out of the car alive, but it won't do any good. He's past hope."

They put me back inside the ambulance and drove away. I vaguely remember when they pulled up at the Huntsville Hospital, a fairly large regional medical center. It was about 2:30 p.m.

By then the authorities had notified my wife, Eva. She teaches school, and someone had called the school to tell her about the accident. Someone else called the schools where our three children attended. Church members picked up our children and took them to their homes to keep them until they heard from Eva.

No one knew then that I had died hours earlier. For the first hours after I returned to earth, they had no idea how extensive my injuries were. Even though they knew nothing specific, church people began to pray for my recovery. They called others to join with them.

Eva found out I had died from Dick Onerecker, almost two weeks after the accident on one of Dick's visits to see me in the hospital. It was only then that she understood just how bad it had been. Also, by that time our insurance agent, Ann Dillman, a member of South Park, had brought pictures of the wreckage after it had been moved from the bridge. Eva says it was quite some time before she really understood how bad it was. She says she probably didn't pay attention to the bad news on purpose because she was trying to focus on immediate matters at hand.

Our children, other family members, and friends then began to piece together just how horrendous the accident was and how close I came to not surviving it.

One of the EMTs said, "We're here now. You're going to be all right."

I was aware of being wheeled into the hospital. I stared uncomprehendingly at a large number of people who pulled back to make space and watched the gurney roll past them. Faces stared down at me, and our eyes met for a split second as the gurney kept moving.

They took me into a room where a doctor was waiting for me. It's strange, but the only thing I recall about the doctor who examined me was that he was bald. He spent quite a while checking me over. "Mr. Piper, we're going to do everything we can to save you," he must have said three times. "You're hurt bad, seriously hurt, but we'll do all we can." Despite his words, I later learned that he didn't expect me to survive. But he did everything he could to give me hope and urge me to fight to stay alive. Several people moved around me. They were obviously trying to save my life, but I still felt no pain. It was like living in some kind of twilight state where I could feel nothing and remained only vaguely aware of what went on around me.

"We have your wife on the phone," someone said. They patched her through on the telephone to the emergency room. A nurse laid the phone beside my ear, and I remember talking to Eva, but I can't recall one word either of us said.

Eva remembers the entire conversation. According to her, the only thing I said was, "I'm so sorry this happened."

"It's okay, Don. It's not your fault."

Over and over I kept saying, "I'm so sorry. I just wanted to come home. Please bring me home." In some kind of childlike way, I suppose I felt that if I couldn't be in my heavenly home, I wanted to be back in my earthly one.

—

I was alert enough to know that they wanted to transport me on a Life Flight helicopter to Hermann Hospital Trauma Center in Houston. But they decided that the weather was too bad and the cloud ceiling too low, so their helicopter couldn't take off.

My condition was deteriorating rapidly, and they didn't know if I was going to survive the afternoon. Despite that, the medical team made a significant decision: They decided to put me back inside an ambulance for the eighty-mile trip to Houston. They didn't have the facilities to take care of me. Hermann Hospital was the only place for me if I was to have any chance to survive.

They brought around a new ambulance. It's amazing that as injured as I was—and they still thought I could "expire" at any second—I became aware of little things such as the fresh odors of a new vehicle, especially the fresh paint.

"You're our first patient," the attendant said as we drove away.

"What?"

"You're the first person to ever ride in this ambulance," he said. "We're going to take you to Houston. We'll get you there as fast as we can."

"How fast do I go?" the driver asked the attendant who sat next to me.

"As fast as you can."

"How fast is that?" the driver asked again.

"Put the pedal to the metal! We've got to get there—*now*!"

Before we started the trip, I still had felt no pain. I was in and out of consciousness. I felt weightless, as if my mind had no connection with my body. However, about ten minutes down the road, a slight throbbing began. At first, I became aware of a tiny pain in my left arm. Then my left leg throbbed. My head started to ache. Within minutes I hurt in so many places, I couldn't localize any of it. My entire body groaned in agony and screamed for relief. The full force of the trauma invaded my body. It felt as if every part of my body had been wounded, punched, or beaten. I couldn't think of a single spot that didn't scream out in pain. I think I cried out but I'm not sure. Every beat of my heart felt like sledgehammers pounding every inch of my body.

"You've got to do something! Please!" I finally pleaded. That much I remember. "Medicine—just something to—"

"I've given you all I can."

"You've given me all you can?" His words didn't make sense. If they'd given me medication, why was I feeling so much pain? "Please—"

"I can't let you go unconscious," the attendant said. "You have to remain awake."

"Please—just something to—"

I couldn't understand why I had to remain awake. If they'd just knock me out, the pain would go away. "Please," I begged again.

"I'm sorry. I really am, but I can't give you anything else. You've already had enough to throw most people into a coma. You're a fairly big guy, but I just can't let you go unconscious."

I'm sure I whimpered, moaned, or even screamed several times during the rest of the torturous ride. The vehicle rocked back and forth, in and out of traffic, and the entire time the siren blared. It was the most painful, nightmarish trip of my life.

Even now I can close my eyes and feel the ambulance vibrating and bumping on the shoulder of the road as it took the curves. One of the EMTs said something about rush-hour traffic just getting heavy, so I assumed it must be around 5:00. Momentarily, I wondered how it could be so late in the day.

The drive seemed interminable, although I think I passed out several times from the pain. We finally arrived at the emergency room in Houston at Hermann Hospital.

It was 6:20 p.m. Six and a half hours had passed from the time of the accident.

By the time I reached the hospital in Houston, thousands of people were praying. They spread the word so that members in hundreds of churches also prayed for my recovery. For the next few days, word spread about my injuries, and more people prayed. Over the years, I've met many of those who asked God to spare my life. Perhaps some of you reading this book prayed for my survival and recovery. I can only add that the prayers were effective: I lived, and I'm still alive.

As the EMTs lifted my gurney out of the ambulance, I spotted Eva's face. Next to her stood a deacon from our church. I felt as if they were looking at some lost puppy, given my pathetic appearance. They were amazed, gawking, but saying nothing.

Eva stared at me. Until that moment, I had been only vaguely aware of what was going on with my body. The pain had not abated, but I still had not reasoned out that I had been in an accident. It didn't occur to me that I was dying.

As I stared into her face, I recognized the anguish in her eyes. She probably said something to try to comfort me, I don't know. What stays with me is that I sensed her pain and that she feared I wouldn't live.

That's when I knew I must have been in really bad shape—and I was. My chest had already turned purple, and medics had bandaged almost every part of my body. Tiny pieces of glass were embedded in my face, chest, and head. I was aware that tiny shards had fallen out of my skin and rested on the gurney next to my head.

No one had to tell me that I looked hideous. Anyone who knew me wouldn't have recognized me. I wondered how Eva had known who I was.

My pain was off the scale. Once inside the trauma center, a nurse gave me a shot of morphine—and then followed up with several more shots. Nothing helped. Nothing dulled the pain.

Shortly after my arrival at Hermann, they sent me to surgery, where I remained for eleven hours. Under anesthesia, I finally felt no pain.

Our dear friend Cliff McArdle valiantly stayed with Eva throughout the night. Cliff, my best friend David Gentiles, and I had been ministry friends since our graduation from seminary and remain close to this day.

By the time I was conscious again, it was Thursday morning. When I opened my eyes, somehow I knew that I had become the first patient in a newly opened ICU pod. One nurse was cleaning my wounds while another was putting me into traction. I could feel that she was putting rods between my ankle and my arm. I heard myself scream.

"We've done an MRI on you," the doctor said. Until then I wasn't aware that he was also in the room. "You're very seriously injured, but the good news is that you have no head or thoracic injuries."

At the time, I didn't care where my injuries were. The throbbing pains were racing through my body. I hurt more than I thought was humanly possible.

I just wanted relief.

—

When Dick Onerecker came to see me two weeks after the accident, I had just been moved from the ICU to a hospital room. He told me about God telling him to pray for me and that he had done that for several minutes.

"The best news is that I don't have any brain damage or any internal injuries," I said.

Dick chuckled. "Of course you don't. That's what God told me to pray for, and God answered."

"You believed that? You believed that God would answer that prayer?"

"Yes, I did," he said. "I knew with all the other injuries you had incurred that God was going to answer my prayer."

It took a few seconds for me to absorb what he'd said. From the force and intensity of the impact, I would have had internal injuries. Even the doctor had commented—in amazement—that I had neither head nor thoracic injuries.

"I'll tell you this," I said. "I know I had internal injuries, but somewhere between that bridge and this hospital I don't anymore."

Tears ran down Dick's face, and he said, "I know. I wish I could pray like that all the time."

6

THE RECOVERY BEGINS

And we can be confident that he will listen to us whenever we ask him for anything in line with his will. And if we know he is listening when we make our requests, we can be sure that he will give us what we ask for.

1 John 5:14–15

Pain became my constant companion. For a long time I would not know what it was like not to hurt all over my body.

Despite that, within a few days of the accident, I began to realize how many miracles had occurred. I refer to them as miracles—although some may call them fortunate circumstances—because I believe there are no accidents or surprises with God.

First, I wore my seat belt. I shamefully admit that I had not "bothered" to wear one until I got ticketed. That morning, I had consciously belted myself in.

Second, the accident happened on the bridge. What if it had happened on the open highway across the lake when I was headed toward the bridge? My car would have plunged down at least thirty feet into the lake, and I would have drowned.

Third, I had no head injuries. Anyone who saw me or read the medical report said it was impossible that I suffered no brain damage. (Eva still jokes that on occasion she's not so sure I didn't.) Just as bewildering to all the medical people was that the accident affected none of my internal organs. That fact defied all medical explanation.

Fourth, orthopedic surgeon Dr. Tom Greider, who was on duty at Hermann Hospital that day, saved my leg. Dr. Greider "just happened to be" one of the few experts in the United States who deals with such bizarre trauma. He chose to use a fairly new, experimental procedure, the Ilizarov frame. He performed the surgery one week after my accident. The implanted Ilizarov not only saved my leg, but also allowed them to lengthen the bone in my left leg after I had lost four inches of my femur in the accident. The femur is the largest bone in the human body and quite difficult to break.

When Dr. Greider examined me, he faced a choice. He could use the Ilizarov frame or amputate. Even if he chose to use the Ilizarov frame, there was no guarantee that I would not lose the leg. In fact, at that stage, he wasn't even certain I would pull through the ordeal. A less-skilled and less-committed doctor might have amputated, assuming it wouldn't make much difference because I would die anyway.

Fifth, people prayed for me. I have thousands of cards, letters, and prayer-grams, many from people I don't know in places I've never been who prayed for me because they heard of the accident. I've since had people tell me that this experience changed their prayer lives and their belief in the power of prayer.

On the night I entered Hermann Trauma Center, I was in surgery for eleven hours. During that operation, I had the broken bone in my right leg set. My left forearm had to be stabilized because two inches of each bone were missing. My left leg was put into traction because four and a half inches of femur were missing. During the operation, an air tube was mistakenly inserted into my stomach. This caused my stomach to inflate and my lungs to deflate. It would be several days before they discovered that this was the cause of the swelling in my stomach. Further complicating my breathing, I was unable to be elevated, and I developed pneumonia. I nearly died a second time.

Because of many bruises and the severity of my obvious wounds, my doctors hardly knew where to start. Other less serious problems became obvious weeks later. Several years passed before they discovered a fractured pelvis that they had missed initially.

I lay on my bed with needles everywhere, unable to move, dependent on the life-support apparatus. I could barely see over the top of my oxygen mask. During most of those days in the ICU, I was in and out of consciousness. Sometimes I'd wake up and see people standing in front of my bed and would wonder, *Am I really here or am I just imagining this?*

Monitors surrounded me, and a pulse oximeter on my finger tracked my oxygen level. Because I wasn't getting enough oxygen, the alarm went off often, bringing nurses racing into my room.

The ICU in Hermann is near the helipad; helicopters took off and landed at all hours of the day. When I was awake, I felt as if I were in a Vietnam movie. There were no clocks in the room, so I had no concept of time.

Other people lay in beds near me, often separated by nothing more than a curtain. More than once I awakened and saw orderlies carrying out a stretcher with a sheet over the body. As a pastor, I knew that many people don't leave the ICU alive.

Am I next? I'd ask myself.

Although I asked the question, the pain prevented my caring. I just wanted not to hurt, and dying would be a quick answer.

I had experienced heaven, returned to earth, and then suffered through the closest thing to hell on earth I ever want to face. It would be a long time before my condition or my attitude changed.

Nightmarish sounds filled the days and the nights. Moans, groans, yells, and screams frequently disrupted my rest and jerked me to consciousness. A nurse would come to my bed and ask, "Can I help you?"

"What are you talking about?" I'd ask. Sometimes I'd just stare at her, unable to understand why she was asking.

"You sounded like you're in great pain."

I am, I'd think, and then I'd ask, "How would you know that?"

"You cried out."

That's when I realized that sometimes the screams I heard came from me. Those groans or yells erupted when I did something as simple as trying to move my hand or my leg. Living in the ICU was horrible. They were doing the best they could, but the pain never let up.

"God, is this what I came back for?" I cried out many times. "You brought me back to earth for this?"

My condition continued to deteriorate. I had to lie flat on my back because of the missing bone in my left leg. (They never found the bone. Apparently, it was ejected from the car into the lake when my leg was crushed between the car seat and dashboard.) Because of having to lie flat, my lungs filled with fluid. Still not realizing my lungs were collapsed, nurses and respiratory therapists tried to force me to breathe into a large plastic breathing device called a spirometer to improve my lung capacity.

On my sixth day, I was so near death that the hospital called my family to come to see me. I had developed double pneumonia, and they didn't think I would make it through the night.

I had survived the injuries; now I was dying of pneumonia. My doctor talked to Eva.

"We're going to have to do something," he told her. "We're either going to have to remove the leg or do something else drastic."

"How drastic?"

"If we don't do something, your husband won't be alive in the morning."

That's when the miracle of prayer really began to work. Hundreds of people had been praying for me since they learned of the accident, and I knew that. Yet, at that point, nothing had seemed to make any difference.

Eva called my best friend, David Gentiles, a pastor in San Antonio. "Please, come and see Don. He needs you," she said.

Without any hesitation, my friend canceled everything and jumped into his car. He drove nearly two hundred miles to see me. The nursing staff allowed him into my room in ICU for only five minutes.

Those minutes changed my life.

I never made this decision consciously, but as I lay there with little hope of recovery—no one had suggested I'd ever be normal again—I didn't want to live. Not only did I face the ordeal of never-lessening pain but I had been to heaven. I wanted to return to that glorious place of perfection. "Take me back, God," I prayed, "please take me back."

Memories filled my mind, and I yearned to stand at that gate once again. "Please, God."

God's answer to that prayer was "no."

When David entered my room, I was disoriented from the pain and the medication. I was so out of it that first I had to establish in my mind that he was real. *Am I hallucinating this?* I asked myself.

Just then, David took my fingers, and I felt his touch. Yes, he was real.

He clasped my fingers because that was all he could hold. I had so many IVs that my veins had collapsed; I had a trunk line that went into my chest and directly to my heart. I used to think of my many IVs as soldiers lined up. I even had IVs in the veins in the tops of my feet. I could look down and see them and realize they'd put needles in my feet because there was no place left on my body.

"You're going to make it," David said. "You have to make it. You've made it this far."

"I don't have to make it. I'm not sure . . . I . . . I don't know if I want to make it."

"You have to. If not for yourself, then hold on for us."

"I'm out of gas," I said. "I've done all I can. I've given it all I can. I don't have anything else to give." I paused and took several breaths, because even to say two sentences sapped an immense amount of energy.

"You have to make it. We won't let you go."

"If I make it, it'll be because all of you want it. I don't want it. I'm tired. I've fought all I can and I'm ready to die."

"Well, then you won't have to do a thing. We'll do it for you."

Uncomprehending, I stared at the intensity on his face.

"We won't let you die. You understand that, Don? We won't let you give up."

"Just let me go—"

"No. You're going to live. Do you hear that? You're going to live. We won't let you die."

"If I live," I finally said, "it'll be because you want me to."

"We're going to pray," he said. Of course, I knew people had been praying already, but he added, "We're going to pray all night. I'm going to call everybody I know who can pray. I want you to know that those of us who care for you are going to stay up all night in prayer for you."

"Okay."

"We're going to do this for you, Don. You don't have to do anything."

I really didn't care whether they prayed or not. I hurt too badly; I didn't want to live.

"We're taking over from here. You don't have to do a thing—not a thing—to survive. All you have to do is just lie there and let it happen. We're going to pray you through this."

He spoke quietly to me for what was probably a minute or two. I don't think I said anything more. The pain intensified—if that was possible—and I couldn't focus on anything else he said.

"We're going to take care of this." David kissed me on the forehead and left.

An all-night prayer vigil ensued. That vigil marked a turning point in my treatment and another series of miracles.

The pneumonia was gone the next day. They prayed it away. And the medical staff discovered the error with the breathing tube.

On that seventh day, in another long surgery, Dr. Greider installed the Ilizarov device so that I could sit up and receive breathing treatments. They also deflated my stomach, which allowed my lungs to inflate.

Normally, hospitals require six months of counseling before they will authorize the use of the Ilizarov frame. In my case, the medical staff could give Eva no guarantee that the experimental procedure would work. They also told her that using the Ilizarov frame would cause me considerable physical pain as well as extraordinary emotional and psychological distress. Worse, they warned that even after going through all of that, I might still lose my leg.

"This is extremely painful and takes months—maybe years—to recover," the surgeon said to Eva. Again he reminded her of the worst that could happen—that I might still lose the leg. "However, if we don't go this route, we have no choice but to amputate."

He quietly explained that if they amputated they would fit me with a prosthesis, and I'd have to learn to walk with it.

Eva had no illusions about the extent of my injury or how long I would have to endure excruciating pain. She debated the pros and cons for several minutes and prayed silently for guidance. "I'll sign the consent form," she finally said.

The next morning, when I awakened after another twelve hours of surgery, I stared at what looked like a huge bulge under the covers where my left leg had been. When I uncovered myself, what I saw took my breath away. On my left leg was a massive stainless steel halo from my hip to just below my knee. A nurse came in and started moving around, doing things around my leg, but I wasn't sure what she did.

I became aware of Eva sitting next to my bed. "What is that?" I asked. "What's she doing?"

"We need to talk about it," she said. "It's what I agreed to yesterday. It's a bone-growth device. We call it a fixator. It's the only chance for the doctors to save your left leg," she said. "I believe it's worth the risk."

I'm not sure I even responded. What was there to say? She had made the best decision she could and had been forced to make it alone.

Just then, I spotted wires leading from the device. "Are those wires going through my leg?"

"Yes."

I shook my head uncomprehendingly. "They're going *through* my leg?"

"It's a new technique. They're trying to save your leg."

I didn't know enough to comment. I nodded and tried to relax.

"I believe it will work," she said.

I hoped she was right. Little did I know that nearly a year later I would still be staring at it.

7

DECISIONS AND CHALLENGES

Can anyone ever separate us from Christ's love? Does it mean he no longer loves us if we have trouble or calamity, or are persecuted, or are hungry or cold or in danger or threatened with death? (Even the Scriptures say, "For your sake we are being killed every day; we are being slaughtered like sheep.")

Romans 8:35–36

One of the most difficult things for me—aside from my own physical pain—was to see the reaction of my family members and close friends. My parents live in Louisiana, about 250 miles from Houston, but they arrived the day after my first surgery. My mother is a strong woman, and I always thought she could handle anything. But she walked into the ICU, stared at me, and then crumpled in a faint. Dad had to grab her and carry her out.

Her collapse made me aware of how pitiful I looked.

Most of those first days remain a blur to me. I wasn't sure if people really visited me or if I only hallucinated—and from what Eva and the nurses told me, I sometimes was delirious.

The hospital allowed visitors to come in each day, a few at a time. Even when they said nothing, their sad, pitying eyes made it clear to me how they felt. I write *clear to me* because I know how I perceived them. In retrospect, I may have been mistaken. I suspect I was so positive I would die—and I wanted to—that I saw in their eyes what I was feeling about myself.

Accurate or not, I felt as if they were staring at a mangled body and not a living person, that despite the assuring and comforting words they spoke, they expected me to die at any moment. I wondered if they had come to pay their last respects before I closed my eyes forever.

Though my pneumonia was gone, we still had to treat its aftermath. Nurses came in every four hours for respiratory therapy treatments. They beat on my chest and forced me to breathe through a plastic mouthpiece an awful-smelling, terrible-tasting stuff that was supposed to coat my lungs. This treatment would prevent the pneumonia from recurring and help restore my lungs. I'd wake up and see people coming in, and I'd think, *Oh no, here we go. They're going to make me breathe that stuff and pound on me and try to get the phlegm dislodged.* As painful as they were, the treatments worked. Dr. Houchins, the head of the Hermann trauma team, came in several times a day. What Dr. Houchins may have lacked in bedside manner, he made up in sheer bulldog determination not to lose any of his patients.

He demanded that I breathe. "Don't quit now. Don't quit. Keep trying." It wasn't just the words he spoke, but—as sick as I was—I felt as if he fought right alongside me. "Don't give up. Keep trying."

Often I didn't have the energy to breathe and just stopped trying.

I saw the pained expression on his face and then watched his features contort into an angry intensity. "Did you hear what I said? Do it! Now! Breathe and cough! Do it!"

I shook my head. I just didn't have the strength to do anything more.

"This is not negotiable. Do this right now! Breathe!"

"I can't."

"All right, don't do it. You're dead. You're going to die if you don't do it. Can you get that into your mind?"

I didn't want to live, but something happened when he yelled at me.

I breathed.

Shortly after that, the staff figured out how to elevate my leg so I could sit up. Just to sit up was a great step forward. I didn't think I'd ever get to lie on my side or stomach again.

Once while I was still in the ICU, it seemed as if every time I opened my eyes and blinked, within seconds someone thrust a spoon filled with food about six inches from my mouth.

"Just open up."

One time it was a man's voice.

I opened my eyes and stared. Holding the spoon was a burly man. He lifted my oxygen mask and gently poked the spoon into my mouth. "That's it, just take a bite."

I obeyed and swallowed while my drugged mind tried to figure out what was going on.

Slowly I realized that the voice belonged to Stan Mauldin, head football coach and athletic director of the Alvin High School Yellow Jackets. Our daughter would live with Stan and Suzan and their two children during my convalescence. Coach Mauldin had heard that because I wouldn't eat, I was losing weight at an alarming rate. (Although I had lost only a few pounds then, within my first six weeks in the hospital I lost nearly fifty pounds.)

As soon as Stan heard about the situation, he made time in his demanding schedule to show up at Hermann Hospital. He didn't just drop in to visit. He asked the nurses to give him my food, and he sat beside my bed until I awakened.

As soon as he realized I was fully awake, Stan shoveled in the food and talked while I did my best to chew and listen. That gentle act of sacrifice by a bear of a man was one of the most thoughtful acts I witnessed during my days of recovery. Stan epitomizes strength and tenderness combined in one exceptional person.

I've referred to the Ilizarov frame, which may have sounded like a common procedure. It was far from that. Eva had to make a decision no one should have to make alone. She had to decide whether to allow the then-experimental Ilizarov process.

Initially this device was used to stretch legs. Its invention came about to help individuals who have a congenital condition where one leg is shorter than the other—some as much as twelve inches—and have to rely on wheelchairs, calipers, or crutches. The Ilizarov frame forces the bone in the leg to grow while keeping the surrounding tissue intact. The body can form new bone between gaps in response to the mechanical force of the Ilizarov frame.

The Ilizarov bone growth device is what they call an external fixator. A Siberian doctor named Ilizarov invented it.

Dr. Ilizarov experimented on sheep to develop a way to grow missing bones or lengthen congenitally short bones. For missing bone cases like mine, the application involves breaking a limb with a clean break. Wires about the size of piano wire are placed through the skin and bone, and they exit out the other side.

The femur Ilizarov device is anchored in the hip by rods about the size of pencils. The doctors drilled holes for four large rods from my groin to the side of my left hip. After they did that, I had at least thirty holes in my left leg. Many of them went completely through my leg and out the other side. The larger ones just went into the flesh, and rods were embedded in the pelvis. After about six months passed, I could actually see down inside my leg as the pinholes stretched out.

Every day someone would come in and turn the screws on the Ilizarov device to stretch the bones. Most of the time the nursing staff took on this task. After I came home, Eva did it. For nearly a year, my left femur bone would regrow and replace the missing piece. It's an ingenious device, although terribly painful, requiring an arduous, lengthy recovery. I called it "hideously wonderful."

Six rods also went through the top of my left arm and came out the other side. Big stainless steel bars were placed above and below the arm to stabilize it, because both forearm bones were missing. The rods were the size of a pencil and allowed Dr. Greider to harvest bones from my right pelvis and place them in my left forearm. The doctor explained that this was like taking core samples when drilling an oil well. They also harvested about thirty-two square inches of skin from my right leg to place over the enormous wound in my left arm. Then they embedded a Teflon strip between the newly constructed bones in my forearm in order to prevent the new bones from adhering to each other—that is, attaching themselves and growing together.

Unfortunately for me, that part of the technique didn't work—the bones healed, but they attached themselves to each other. Consequently, I have no pronation or supination in my left arm—my arm does not straighten out at the elbow, and I can't turn palms up or palms down. When I extend my arm, my hand is always in a hand-shaking position. My hand cannot twist either right or left. I know all this seems barbaric, and at the time it felt like it. But like the Ilizarov, it works.

Yes, the Ilizarov device worked—and it was also the most painful process I endured as part of my recovery.

The stainless steel Ilizarov on my leg weighed about thirty pounds, and the external fixator on my arm probably weighed another twenty. Whether I was in my wheelchair (about eight months), on my rolling walker (three more months), or eventually my crutches (four more months), I carried that extra weight around for nearly a year.

Can you imagine the strange stares I received everywhere I went? People gasped and gawked at a man in a wheelchair with steel rods sticking out all over his body.

Virtually every time I made my routine visit to Dr. Greider's office in my wheelchair, the reaction of the other patients was universal. Though each wore casts or braces or walked on crutches, all of them would stare at me and my rods and halos. Then without fail, someone would say somewhat sardonically, "Wow, and I thought I was bad off." Occasionally, someone would even add, "After seeing you, I feel better." For a long time, I became the standard by which painful injury was judged.

I've often kidded others that because of all this "metalwork," if archaeologists discover my body years from now, they'll think they've found a new species! My anatomy has been completely rearranged.

Never again will I take simple physical ability for granted. During my recovery, even the tiniest movement was a miracle. Every time I relearned how to do something, it felt like an achievement.

Only later did I understand how hard Dr. Greider had worked to find a way to save my left leg and arm. I'll always be grateful that he didn't just give up on me.

My right knee was crushed, and I wore a cast on it for quite some time. They put a small, mesh basket around the kneecap so it would heal. My right arm was the only limb that didn't break.

Even with the success of the Ilizarov frame, however, the pain didn't leave—not for one minute.

81

I wonder how many times I asked, "How long?" I wanted to know how long I'd have to endure the device, how long before I'd know if it worked, how long before I'd walk again.

No one would—or could—give me an answer, but I kept asking anyway.

"A few months," was the usual answer.

"How few?" I persisted.

One of the doctors finally said, "Many months. Maybe longer."

"You mean possibly a few years?"

"Yes, perhaps years."

"And there's no guarantee that I'm going to be able to keep these limbs?"

"There's no guarantee. An infection could come on suddenly, and we'd be forced to remove your leg."

"You mean I could endure this for months and still end up with no leg?"

He nodded.

Obviously, that wasn't what I wanted to hear. Even though Eva had told me the same thing, denial must have set in. I kept seeking a guarantee that I would fully recover.

I wanted answers, but perhaps even more than that, I wanted assurance that I would be well. I wanted to be normal again. I wanted to be able to walk out of the hospital on my own two legs and go back to my former way of life. No one was willing—or able—to give me those assurances.

Many months passed, but one day I did walk back into that hospital and hug all those nurses.

During the months after I received the Ilizarov frame, I had other problems. I developed infections—several times. Each time, I faced the reality that it might rage through my body and I would wake up without my leg.

I also had infections after they released me. Three times I had to be rehospitalized, put in isolation, and receive massive amounts of antibiotics to cure the infections.

Even then, many nights I prayed, *God, take me back to heaven. I don't know why you brought me back to earth. Please don't leave me here.*

God's answer to that prayer was still "no."

I still don't know all the reasons, but in the months and years ahead, I slowly understood at least some of the reasons I had returned to earth.

~

The healing process had begun. As I lay in that hospital bed day after day, I slowly acknowledged that God had sent me back to earth. I couldn't figure out why I had to endure the physical suffering, but I kept thinking of the words of David Gentiles. He and others had cried out in prayer for me to live. Because God had answered them, there had to be a purpose in my staying alive.

Through days of intense agony, I would remember David's words. Sometimes the sense that God had a purpose in my being alive was all that kept me going.

I was in Hermann ICU for twelve days. Then I stayed four to five days in Hermann Hospital before they transferred me down the street to St. Luke's Hospital. Both hospitals are part of the world's largest medical center. I remained in St. Luke's for 105 days. Once I was home, I lay in bed for thirteen months and endured thirty-four surgeries. Without question, I am still alive because people prayed for me, beginning with Dick Onerecker and other people around the country, many of whom I've never met.

That's perhaps the biggest miracle: *People prayed and God honored their prayers.*

As I look back, I see how many people God used to save me. Dick Onerecker saved my life by his continued praying. Dr. Greider saved my leg and my arm and got me through that initial surgery. Dr. Houchins saved my life after the surgery because of his bulldog determination to keep me alive. The courageous nurses of the orthopedic floor of St. Luke's Hospital cared for me day and night. Each of them played a vital role.

I attribute leaving ICU alive to the prayers of David Gentiles and the others. "We're taking over from here. You don't have to do a thing to survive. We're going to pray you through this."

I knew I wasn't going to die.

God's people wouldn't let me.

8

PAIN AND ADJUSTMENTS

Don't be afraid, for I am with you. Do not be dismayed, for I am your God. I will strengthen you. I will help you. I will uphold you with my victorious right hand.

Isaiah 41:10

Even though they didn't realize it, visitors made my situation worse. They cared for me and wanted to express that concern. Because they cared, they did the most natural thing in the world—they visited my hospital room. That was the problem.

The constant flow in and out of my room exhausted me. I couldn't just lie there and allow them to sit with me or talk at me. Maybe I needed to function in my role as pastor or felt some kind of obligation to entertain them. I didn't want to hurt anyone's feelings by asking him or her to leave or not to come.

Many days, I smiled and chatted with them when all I really wanted to do was collapse. Sometimes the intense pain made it almost impossible for me to be a good host, but I still tried to be gracious. I kept reminding myself that they cared and had made an effort to see me.

Between friends, relatives, and church members, I felt as if a line stretched from the front door of the hospital to my room. Eva came in one afternoon and realized how much the visitors disturbed me. She chided me for allowing it.

I think she figured out that I wouldn't tell anyone not to come back, so she asked the nursing staff to cut back on the number of visitors they allowed. It didn't stop everyone from coming, but it did cut down the traffic in and out of the room.

Besides the pain and the flow of people in and out of my room, I lived in depression. A large part of it may have been the natural result of the trauma to my body and some of it may have been my reaction to the many drugs. I believe, however, that because I faced an unknown outcome and the pain never let up, I kept feeling I had little future to look forward to. Most of the time I didn't want to live.

Why was I brought back from a perfect heaven to live a pain-filled life on earth? No matter how hard I tried, I couldn't enjoy living again; I wanted to go back to heaven.

Pain has become a way of life for me since the accident, as I am sure it has for many. It's curious that we can learn to live with such conditions. Even now, on rare occasions when I am lying in bed after a good night's sleep, I will suddenly notice that I don't hurt anywhere. Only then am I reminded that I live in continuous pain the other twenty-three hours and fifty-five minutes of each day.

It took a while for me to realize how profoundly my condition affected my emotions.

I prayed and others prayed with me, but a sense of despair began to set in. "Is it worth all this?" I asked several times every day.

The doctors and nurses kept trying to push medications on me for my depression, but I refused. I'm not sure why. Perhaps because I had so much medicine in me, I didn't want any more. Besides, I didn't think more medicine would do any good.

I wanted to be free from my miserable existence and die. Obviously, I felt wholly unequipped to deal with that turn of events. I now know that I was a textbook depression case.

Soon everyone else knew it too.

"Would you like to talk to a psychiatrist?" my doctor asked.

"No," I said.

A few days later, one of the nurses asked, "Would you like me to call in a therapist? Someone you could talk to?"

My answer was the same.

Because I didn't want to talk to anyone, what I called "stealth shrinks" began to creep into my room.

"I see you've been in a very severe accident," one undercover psychiatrist said after reading my chart. He tried to get me to talk about how I felt.

"I don't want to talk about the accident," I said. The truth is, I couldn't. How could I possibly explain to anyone what had happened to me during the ninety minutes I was gone from this earth? How could I find words to express the inexpressible? I didn't know how to explain that I had literally gone to heaven. I was sure that if I started talking that way, he'd know I was crazy. He'd think something had gone dreadfully wrong with my mind, that I had hallucinated, or that I needed stronger drugs to take away my delusions. How could I put into words that I had had the most joyful, powerful experience of my life? How could I sound rational by saying I preferred to die? I knew what was waiting, but he didn't.

I had no intention of talking to a psychiatrist (or anyone else) about what had happened to me. I saw that experience as something too intimate, too intense to share. As close as Eva and I are, I couldn't even tell her at that time.

Going to heaven had been too sacred, too special. I felt that talking about my ninety minutes in heaven would defile those precious moments. I never doubted or questioned whether my trip to heaven had been real. That never troubled me. Everything had been so vivid and real, I couldn't possibly deny it. No, the problem was I didn't want to share that powerful experience with anyone.

That didn't stop the psychiatrists from coming into my room and trying to help me. After a few times, they didn't tell me they were psychiatrists. It's humorous now, but the hospital psychiatrists were determined to help me. After I refused to talk to them, they would sneak into my room and observe me. Sometimes they came in while a nurse was working on me. Other times they came in and studied my chart and said nothing, and I assumed they expected me to start a conversation.

Often they'd walk in and say something like, "I'm Dr. Jones," but nothing else. The doctor might check my pulse and ask, "How's your stomach?" He'd examine my chart and ask pertinent questions. Eventually, he'd give himself away with a simple question such as "How do you feel today?"

"About the same."

"How do you really feel about all of this?" No matter how they varied the routine, they always asked how I *really* felt.

"You're a psychiatrist, aren't you?" I'd ask.

"Well, uh, actually, yes."

"Okay, what do you want to know? You want to know if I'm depressed? The answer is I'm very depressed. And I don't want to talk about it."

The conversations went on, but I've blotted most of them from my mind. Even though I knew Dr. Jones and the others were trying to help me, I didn't believe there was any hope. I hated being depressed, but I didn't know what to do about it.

The longer I lay in bed, the more convinced I became that I had nothing to look forward to. Heaven had been perfect—so beautiful and joyful. I wanted to be released from pain and go back.

"Why would anyone want to stay here after experiencing heaven?" I asked God. "Please, please take me back."

I didn't die, and I didn't get over my depression.

I didn't just refuse to talk to psychiatrists; I didn't want to talk to anyone about anything. I didn't want to see anyone. I would have been fine if no one visited me—or so I told myself.

In my depression, I just wanted to be left alone so I could die alone, without anyone trying to resuscitate me.

I also had enough pride as a professional and as a pastor that I didn't want anyone to see how bad off I was. I don't mean just the physical problems; I didn't want them to know about my low emotional state either.

When people did get into the room to see me, of course, their words and gazes made me feel as if they were saying, "You're the most pitiful thing I've ever seen."

I guess I was.

And so the depression continued. It would be a long time before God would give me another miracle.

———

I was the father of three children, the husband of a wonderful wife, and until the accident, a man with a great future. I was thirty-eight years old when the accident happened and until then, the picture of health and in great physical shape. Within days after my accident, I knew I would never be that virile, healthy man again. Now I was utterly helpless. I couldn't do anything for myself, not even lift my hand. Deep inside, I feared I would be helpless for the rest of my life.

As an example of my helplessness, I had not had a bowel movement for the first twelve days in the hospital. Knowing my system would turn septic, they gave me an enema, but that didn't do much good.

I say "not much good" because I would pass a tiny amount and the nurse or nursing assistant would smile with delight.

One day I managed to squeeze out a tiny bit. "Oh, that's so good. We're so happy for you. Let's wait. Maybe there'll be more."

In my depression, I'd think, *This is the most pitiful experience in my life. I'm like a baby and everybody gets excited over a tiny bowel movement.*

I don't remember what I said to the nursing assistant, but I'm sure I wasn't pleasant.

She left the room. That was one of those rare times when no one was visiting. I was totally alone and glad for the peace and quiet.

Within minutes after the nurse left, the enema took effect.

I exploded. I had the biggest bowel movement I've ever had in my life. The odor overwhelmed me.

In my panic, I clawed through the sheet and my fingers finally found the call button. Seconds later, the young nursing assistant raced into the room.

"I'm so sorry, I didn't mean to do this," I said. "I'll help you clean it up." The words had no sooner left my mouth before I realized I couldn't help her. I felt terrible, helpless, and loathsome.

I started to cry.

"No, no, no, don't worry about a thing. We're just so happy that you did it. This is good because it means your system is beginning to work again."

In humiliation, I could only lie there and watch the poor young woman change everything. It must have taken her at least half an hour to clean up and then at least twice that long for the odor to vanish.

My embarrassment didn't leave me, even though my mind tried to tell me differently. I had barely taken in any food for twelve days and this was a real breakthrough. I, however, could only think that this was one of the most embarrassing events in my life.

As awful as it seemed to me, more embarrassing, helpless experiences caught up with me. I had to have a urinal; I couldn't wipe myself; I couldn't shave. I couldn't even wash my hair. They had to bring special devices to lay my head in and pour water over my hair and then drain it down a tube to a garbage can. In yet another act of incredible kindness, Carol Benefield, who had cut my hair for years, came to trim my hair several times while I was confined to my bed. For these sixty-mile round-trips, Carol would accept no money whatsoever.

Friends, family, and medical personnel found ways of providing for all of my physical needs, but I could only think of myself as being completely, utterly helpless. My right arm, the one that hadn't been broken, had so many IVs in it that they had a piece of wood taped to me so I couldn't bend the arm.

I had IVs everywhere. They ran into my chest and entered the tops of my feet. They lined up in a major tube that went directly to my heart through my chest. Many of my veins collapsed. I was so completely incapacitated they had to lift me off the bed with chains to change my bedding or do anything else that required moving me.

I was losing weight at an alarming rate, which scared the doctors. I just couldn't eat anything and atrophy had set in. During the nearly four months I stayed in the hospital, I lost about sixty pounds. Before the accident I had weighed 210, and I got down to less than 150. The only way they could determine my weight was to put me in a sling like a baby to lift me up off the bed and weigh me. They tried to coax me into eating and tempted me by preparing my favorite foods, but nothing tasted good. Just the smell of food nauseated me. I had no appetite. I tried to eat, I really did, but I couldn't handle more than a few bites.

I assumed that depression stopped me from eating, although I don't know if that was the cause. I do know that when I tried, I couldn't force myself to chew anything. I didn't even want to swallow.

They attached me to a morphine pump they called a PC. Whenever the pain was really bad, I pushed a button to give myself a shot. I had to have pain medication constantly. At first I tried to resist taking more painkillers, but the doctor rebuked me for that. He said that my body was tensing from the pain and that retarded my healing.

At night they gave me additional medication to try to make me sleep. I write *try* because the additional medicine didn't work. Nothing they did put me to sleep—not sleeping pills, pain shots, or additional morphine. I had no way to get comfortable or even to feel relieved enough from pain to relax.

I've tried to explain it by saying it this way: "Imagine yourself lying in bed, and you've got rods through your arms, wires through your legs, and you're on your back. You can't turn over. In fact, just to move your shoulder a quarter of an inch is impossible unless you reach up and grab what looks like a trapeze bar that hangs above your bed. Even the exertion to move a fraction of an inch sends daggers of pain all through your body. You are completely immobile."

Because I began to break out with bedsores on my back due to being in one position too long, the hospital finally provided a special waterbed that constantly moved. That did take care of the bedsores.

The only time I ever left the room was when they wheeled me down to X-ray, which was always an adventure. Because of all the metal parts and equipment on me, they had trouble figuring out how to x-ray me. Three or four men wore lead suits in the X-ray room and held the lens and plates behind my steel-encased limbs, because no machine was designed to x-ray those types of things.

That also meant that some days I spent two or three hours in X-ray while the technicians tried to figure out how to take a picture so the doctors could see whether the bones were knitting. They had no precedent for a case such as mine.

When someone came to wheel me to X-ray, he'd always say, "We're taking a trip down the hall."

That was all they had to say, because I knew what they meant. To distract myself as the gurney cruised down the long hallways, I played a game of connect-the-dots with the ceiling tiles. I started that the day I came back from the first surgery. I was probably hallucinating, but I remember the ICU unit was brand-new, and I was the only patient. When they brought me in, I was moaning and couldn't stop. Then I saw the ceiling tiles, and as I stared at them, it seemed as if they were running together and forming some kind of pattern that I couldn't figure out. In my mind, I began making pictures and designs out of them. As I did that, I'd also think, *I'm going completely crazy.* But I did it anyway. Eventually, connecting the dots became a form of distraction allowing me to focus, if only momentarily, on something other than my pain.

The worst daily torment took place when a nurse cleaned the pinholes where the wires went into my skin. All the nurses that treated me on the orthopedic floor, the twenty-first floor of St. Luke's Hospital, had to be taught how to clean those pinholes. Because they didn't want the skin to adhere to the wire, they had to keep breaking the skin when it attached itself—as it did occasionally. Then the nurse forced hydrogen peroxide down each pinhole to prevent infection. I could think of nothing worse to endure, and it happened every day.

That wasn't all. Four times a day, every six hours, they'd take an Allen wrench and turn screws on the device. The idea was that this would stretch the ends of the bones inside the leg and eventually cause the growing bone to replace the missing bone.

The turn hurt beyond description, even though each turn was very slight, less than half a millimeter. It didn't matter whether it was day or night, every six hours someone came into my room to turn the screws.

As a pastor, I had visited many hospital rooms, including trips to the ICU. I had seen agony on many faces, and I had frequently winced in sympathy. Even so, I couldn't imagine anything on a day-to-day basis that could be more painful.

Perhaps the worst part for me was that I never slept. For eleven and a half months I never went to sleep—I just passed out. Even with megadoses of morphine, I was never pain free. When they decided it was time for me to go to sleep, a nurse injected me with three or four shots of either morphine or another sleeping medicine. I'd lie in bed, and no matter how much I told myself to relax, I couldn't. I fought the pain and then, apparently, I passed out. My next conscious moment would be an awareness of intense pain. I felt nothing else in between.

Eventually, family members and even hospital personnel left me alone because they knew I didn't have a functioning body clock. I had no sense of time, and I couldn't relax, because I was under such tension. If I made the slightest effort to move, a wire embedded in my flesh would tear my skin at the point of entry. I could move, but the wires didn't. With even the tiniest movement, excruciating pain slashed through my entire body.

After a while, I learned to live with that situation, but I never got used to it.

The first person I "met" (we never saw each other in person) for whom the Ilizarov frame was used for its original purpose was Christy. The Ilizarov procedure was created to lengthen bones for people born with congenital birth defects. However, the device could not be attached until the bones had stopped growing.

Especially during adolescence, bones grow at a very rapid pace, so doctors must carefully choose the right time for the procedure.

Christy, a teenage girl, was in the room next to mine. She had been born with one leg shorter than the other. Once her bones had matured, she had chosen surgery to attach the Ilizarov frame to have her bones lengthened so that both legs would be of normal size.

Because Christy's surgery was elective, she had some idea about the pain and the length of recovery she would have to go through. For months, she had gone through extensive counseling, and her family knew how to take care of the wounds. They also knew approximately how long it would take and the commitment they had to make to care for her.

The difference between Christy and me was that she knew what she was getting into—at least to the extent that anyone can. I woke up with the device already attached. In my depressed state, that made me feel even worse. Even though I knew they had put the Ilizarov frame on me to save my leg, I could only see it as the major source of my agony.

Another problem arose, although a minor one. Even though we had different doctors, the same staff people came into Christy's room and mine to turn the screws. Sometimes the wrenches got misplaced, and the attendant couldn't find them in my room so they'd rush over to Christy's for hers. Or they'd come and borrow mine. Fortunately for both of us, our fixators were interchangeable and someone could borrow wrenches from one room to adjust screws in the other room.

That's how I first learned about Christy—the borrowing of wrenches. We never saw each other face-to-face, but we did see each other's doctor, and somehow that, plus our common problem, created a bond between us.

Christy and I shared something else—pain. Many times I heard her crying. I don't mean weeping, but a cry, or a scream, and sometimes just a low moan. She probably heard similar sounds from my room as well. I wasn't as likely to cry because that's not my nature. One of the nurses suggested it might be better if I did let go and scream. Even though she may have been right, I never did—at least not consciously.

When I was in control of my faculties, I never cried out. I had heard others scream from their pain and their cries disturbed me greatly. Also, I had learned to keep my hurts and emotions to myself. I believed at that time that moans, wails, and screams did no good. The only times I screamed, I was either unconscious or heavily medicated. I learned about those outbursts because other people told me.

Although Christy and I never met during the twelve weeks we lived next door to each other, we corresponded by sending letters back and forth, and the nurses willingly acted as our mail carriers.

I tried to encourage Christy. She told me her story and was very sympathetic to my accident. She was also a believer. We corresponded on that level as well.

In some of my worst moments of self-pity, however, I would think that when all the pain was over, Christy would be a normal young woman; I would never be normal again. She could play and run and do everything a normal teen did. Even then I knew I would never run again.

I had many, many times of self-pity, reminding myself that she chose her pain, while I had no warning and no options. She knew in advance what she was getting into; I had no idea. She was doing something that positively impacted the rest of her life; I was doing something just to save my life. Yes, self-pity filled my mind many, many days.

Always, however, I came back to one thing: God had chosen to keep me alive. Even in my worst moments of depression and self-pity, I never forgot that.

Christy and I shared similar pain. We also shared a faith that reminded us that our loving God was with us in the most terrible moments of suffering. Just having her in the next room comforted me, because I'd think, *I'm not the only one; somebody else understands how I feel.*

That's when I began to think of being part of an exclusive fraternity. In the years since my release, I've met other members of this reluctant and small fellowship. Because I knew what it felt like to suffer, I could understand their pain, just as Christy had felt mine and I had understood hers.

More than enduring, eventually I was able to do something doctors said I would never be able to do: I learned to walk again. I can stand on my own feet, put one foot in front of the other, and move.

They had warned me that because of the broken knee in my right leg, and the loss of the femur in my left (even with a replaced-and-stretched bone in place), I would not walk again, and if I did, I would be wearing heavy braces. More than once, I came close to losing my left leg, but somehow God took me through each crisis.

Therapy began on my arm about four weeks after the initial operation and on my legs two weeks after that.

About the same time, they put me in what I referred to as a Frankenstein bed. They strapped me to a large board and turned the bed so that my feet were on the floor and I was in a standing position, although still strapped to the bed. Two physical therapists placed a large belt around my waist and walked on either side of me. My legs had atrophied and grown extremely weak, so they helped me take my first steps. It took me days to learn to stand again so that I could put weight on my own legs. My equilibrium had changed because I had grown used to a horizontal position. I became incredibly nauseous each time they raised me into a vertical position. Days passed before I was used to that position enough to take my first step.

I didn't really learn to walk until after the hospital discharged me. A physical therapist came in every other day to help me. Six months would pass before I learned to walk on my own more than a few steps.

My doctor removed the Ilizarov device eleven and a half months after the accident. After that, I could use a walker and eventually a cane. I didn't walk without leg braces and a cane for a year and a half after the accident.

My accident occurred in January 1989. They removed the external metal work from my arm fixator in May, but they put internal metal plates down both of the bones of the forearm. Those metal plates stayed there for several more months.

In late November, they removed the fixator from my leg, but that wasn't the end. After that, I remained in a cast for a long time, and they inserted a plate in my leg—which stayed there for nine years. I was content to leave it there, but they said they had to take it out. My doctor explained that as I aged, the bones, relying on the plate for strength, would become brittle. As I learned, our bones become and remain strong only as a result of tension and use.

During those years with the fixator and the subsequent metal plates, whenever I had to fly, I set off metal detectors from Ohio to California. Rather than go through the customary walk-through detector, I would say to the security people, "I have more stainless steel in me than your silverware drawer at home."

They would wand me and smile. "You sure do."

My children took pride in referring to me as "Robopreacher" after the title character in the movie *Robocop*. After a horrible incident, doctors used high technology and metal plates to restore the policeman so he could fight crime.

Regardless of how barbaric all these rods and wires and plates might have seemed, they worked. People gasped when they saw them embedded in my flesh. Those same people are now awed at my mobility. But under this thin veneer of normalcy, I'm still a work in progress, always adjusting.

9

ENDLESS ADJUSTMENTS

A friend is always loyal, and a brother is born to help in time
of need.

Proverbs 17:17

It's amazing how differently people responded after the accident. Several friends and members of South Park Church
saw me during those first five days after my accident. Many
of those same people saw me after the all-night prayer vigil
that David Gentiles instigated. As they watched each tiny step
of my recovery, they rejoiced. I saw everything in my recovery
happening so slowly that acute depression continually gripped
me. After the ICU, I stayed in the hospital 105 days the first
time. I suppose depression would strike anyone who has been
confined that long.

During the months of my recovery, the church worked hard
to make me feel useful. They brought vanloads of kids to the
hospital to see me. Sometimes committees met in my hospital
room—as if I could make any decisions. They knew I couldn't

say or do much, but it was their way to affirm and encourage me. They did everything they could to make me feel worthwhile and useful.

Much of that time, however, I was depressed and filled with self-pity. I yearned to go back to heaven.

~

Beyond the depression, I had another problem: I didn't want anybody to do anything for me. That's my nature.

One day Jay B. Perkins, a retired minister, came to visit me. He had served as pastor of several south Texas churches before his retirement and had become a powerful father figure in the ministry for me. South Park hired him as the interim while I was incapacitated.

Jay visited me faithfully. That meant he had to drive more than forty miles each way. He came often to see me, sometimes two or three times a week. I wasn't fit company, but I smiled each time anyway. I'd lie in bed and feel sorry for myself. He'd speak kindly, always trying to find words to encourage me, but nothing he said helped—although that wasn't his fault. No one could help me. Not only was I miserable but, as I learned later, I made everyone else miserable.

My visitors tried to help me, and many wanted to do whatever they could for me. "Can I get you a magazine?" someone would ask.

"Would you like a milkshake? There's a McDonald's in the lobby. Or I could get you a hamburger or . . ."

"Would you like me to read the Bible to you? Or maybe some other book?"

"Are there any errands I can run for you?"

My answer was always the same: "No, thanks."

I don't think I was mean, but I wasn't friendly or cooperative, although I wasn't aware of how negatively I treated everyone.

I didn't want to see anyone; I didn't want to talk to anyone; I wanted my pain and disfigurement to go away. If I had to stay on earth, then I wanted to get well and get back to living my life again.

Because Jay visited often, he noticed how detached I was from friends and family. One day he was sitting beside me when one of the South Park deacons came for a visit. After ten minutes, the man got up and said, "I just wanted to come by and check on you." Then he asked the inevitable question, "Is there anything I can get for you before I leave?"

"Thank you, no. I appreciate it, but—"

"Well, can I get you something to eat? Can I go downstairs and—"

"No, really. Thanks for coming."

He said good-bye and left.

Jay sat silently and stared out the window for several minutes after the deacon left. Finally he walked over to the bed and got close to my face and said, "You really need to get your act together."

"Sir?" I said like anyone would say respectfully to an eighty-year-old preacher.

"You need to get your act together," he repeated. "You're just not doing a very good job."

"I don't understand what—"

"Besides that," he said and moved even closer so that I couldn't look away. "Besides that, you're a raging hypocrite."

"I don't know what you're talking about."

"These people care about you so much, and you just can't imagine how deeply they love you."

"I know they love me."

"Really? Well, you're not doing a very good job of letting them know you're aware. You're not treating them right. They can't heal you. If they could heal you, they would do it. If they could

102

change places with you, many of them would. If you ask them to do anything—anything—they would do it without hesitating."

"I know—"

"But you won't let them do anything for you."

"I don't *want* them to do anything." Without holding anything back, I said as loudly as I could, "The truth is I don't even want them to be here. I'd just as soon they didn't come. I know it's inconvenient. They must have better things to do. I know that—why would I want anybody to come and see me like this? It's just awful. I'm pathetic."

"It's not your call."

I stared back, shocked at his words.

"You've spent the better part of your life trying to minister to other people, to meet their needs, to help them during times of difficulty and tragedy and—"

"I . . . I've tried to—"

"And now you're doing a terrible job of letting these people do the same thing for you." I'll never forget the next sentence. *"Don, it's the only thing they have to offer you, and you're taking that gift away from them."*

Not ready to surrender, I protested and tried to explain. He interrupted me again.

"You're not letting them minister to you. It's what they want to do. Why can't you understand that?"

I really didn't get the impact of his words, but I said, "I appreciate them, and I know they want to help. I think that's very fine and everything but—"

"But nothing! You're cheating them out of an opportunity to express their love to you."

His words shocked me. In my thinking, I was trying to be selfless and not impose on them or cause them any trouble. Just then, his words penetrated my consciousness. In reality, I was being selfish. There was also an element of pride there—which

I couldn't admit then. I knew how to give generously to others, but pride wouldn't let me receive others' generosity.

Jay didn't let up on me. After all, I was a completely captive audience. He stayed at me until he forced me to see how badly I distanced myself from everyone. Even then I found additional excuses, but Jay wore me down.

"I want you to let them help you. Did you hear me? You will allow them to help!"

"I can't—I just can't let—"

"Okay, Don, then if you don't do it for yourself, do this for *me*," he said.

He knew I'd do anything for him, so I nodded.

"The next time anyone comes in here and offers to do something—anything, no matter what it is—I want you to say yes. You probably can't do that with everyone, but you can start with just one or two people. Let a few of the people express their love by helping you. Promise me you'll do that."

"I'm not sure I can."

"Yes, you can."

"I'll try, but that's just not me."

"Then make it you." His gaze bored into me. "Do it!"

I'm amazed now as I think of Jay's patience with me. His voice softened, and he said, "Just try it for me, would you? You have to get better at this. Right now you're not doing very well. This is one of the lessons God wants you to learn. You're going to be hurting a long time. It'll feel longer if you keep on refusing help."

"Okay," I said, unable to resist any longer.

I promised. I didn't think he would leave until I did.

My first reaction had been irritation, maybe even anger. I thought he had stepped over the line, but I didn't say that. After he left, I thought about all the things he had said. Once I overcame my anger, my pride, and my selfishness, I realized he had spoken the truth—truth I needed to hear.

Two days passed, and I still couldn't do what he asked.

On the third day, a church member popped into my room, greeted me, and spent about five minutes with me before he got up to leave. "I just wanted to come by and check on you and see how you were doing," he said. "You're looking good."

I smiled; I looked terrible, but I didn't argue with him.

He stood up to leave. "Is there anything I can do for you before I go?"

I had my mouth poised to say the words, "No, thank you," and an image of Jay popped into my mind. "Well, I wish I had a magazine to read."

"You do?" He had the biggest grin on his face. "Really?"

"I think so. I haven't read one in a while—"

"I'll be right back!" Before I could tell him what kind, he dashed out the door so fast it was like a human blur. He had to go down twenty-one floors, but it seemed as if he were gone less than a minute. When he returned, he had an armload of magazines. He was still grinning as he showed me the covers of all of them.

I thanked him. "I'll read them a little later," I said.

He put them on the table and smiled. "Is there anything else?"

"No, no, that's all I need. Thank you."

Once I had opened the door and allowed someone to do something kind for me, I realized it wasn't so hard after all. After he left, I began skimming through the magazines. I wasn't really reading, because I kept thinking about what had happened.

Jay was right. I had cheated them out of the opportunity to express their love and concern.

About forty minutes later, a woman from the singles group came to see me, and we went through the regular ritual of chatting. "How are you doing?"

"Fine."

"Well, can I get you anything?"

"No, I . . . I—" Again, Jay's words popped into my head. "Well, maybe a strawberry milkshake."

"Strawberry milkshake? I'd love to get one for you." I don't think I had ever seen her smile so beautifully before. "Anything else? Some fries, maybe?"

"No."

She dashed out the door and came back with the strawberry milkshake. "Oh, Pastor, I hope you enjoy this."

"I will," I said. "As a matter of fact, I love strawberry milkshakes."

Later, I imagined members of the congregation standing outside my door comparing notes. "He asked me to get a strawberry milkshake."

"Yes, and he let me run an errand for him."

Just then I realized how badly I had missed the whole idea. I had failed them and myself. In trying to be strong for them, I had cheated them out of opportunities to strengthen me. Guilt overwhelmed me, because I could—at last—see their gifts to me.

The shame flowed all over me, and I began to cry. *This is their ministry*, I thought, *and I've been spoiling it.* I felt such intense shame over not letting them help. When I finally did open up, I witnessed a drastic change in their facial expressions and in their movements. They loved it. All they had wanted was a chance to do something, and I was finally giving that to them.

You need to get your act together. For the next several hours those words of loving rebuke from Jay wouldn't go away. Tears flowed. I have no idea how much time passed, but it seemed hours before I finally realized God had forgiven me. I had learned a lesson.

In spite of my condition, not many people could have pulled off what Jay did. That experience changed my attitude. Even now, years later, I still fight with allowing others to help, but at least the door is now ajar instead of locked shut.

Sometimes when I'm emotionally low or physically down, I tend to brush people off or assert that I don't need anything. Yet when I can open up and allow others to exercise their gifts and help me, it makes such a difference. Their faces light up as if they're asking, "Will you really let me do that for you?"

I had seen my refusal as not wanting to impose; they saw my change as giving them an opportunity to help.

I'm eternally grateful for that lesson of allowing people to meet my needs. I'm also grateful because that lesson was learned in a hospital bed when I was helpless.

Someone brought a plaque to me in the hospital. At first, I thought it was supposed to be some kind of joke because it contained the words of Psalm 46:10: "Be still, and know that I am God" (NIV). Perhaps it was meant to console me. I'm not sure the person who gave it to me (and I don't remember who it was) realized that I couldn't do anything *but* be still.

Yet that plaque contained the message I needed; it just took me a long time to understand.

Weeks lapsed before I realized that part of what I needed was to be still—inwardly—and to trust that God knew what he was doing through all of this. Yes, it was a verse for me, even though it wasn't one I would have chosen.

God forced me to be still. By nature I'm not particularly introspective, but I became increasingly so; I had no choice. I could do little else—other than feel sorry for myself. The longer I lay immobile, the more open I became to God's quietness and to inner silence.

Eva found a beautiful version of that same verse engraved in gold and gave it to me as a gift. The plaque is now in my church office; I see it every time I look up from my desk.

Day after day I lay in bed, unable to move. I lay on my back a total of thirteen months before I could turn over on my side. Just that simple action made it one of the best days of recovery. "Oh, I had forgotten how good this feels," I said aloud.

During that long recovery, I learned a lot about myself, about my attitude, and my nature. I didn't like many things I saw in Don Piper. In the midst of that inactivity, however, the depression persisted.

I began to wonder if that depression would ever go away.

Then God provided another miracle.

10

MORE MIRACLES

I will praise the LORD at all times.
   I will constantly speak his praises.
I will boast only in the LORD;
   let all who are discouraged take heart.
Come, let us tell of the LORD's greatness;
   let us exalt his name together.
I prayed to the LORD, and he answered me,
   freeing me from all my fears.

Psalm 34:1–4

Sometimes the depression became so bad I didn't think I could breathe. It carried me back to the days in the ICU when I received breathing treatments because my lungs had collapsed. Except now my lungs weren't collapsed, only my spirit. Few things sap the human spirit like lack of hope. For weeks and months, no one could tell me when or even if I would ever be normal again. As a result, I went into a full-scale depression.

As my horribly mangled body mended, I needed spiritual mending as well. I began to think of it this way: The Greek word for "spirit" is *pneuma*. The word can also mean "wind" or "breath." That Greek word is the root for what we call *pneumonia*. Just as it was necessary to reinflate my lungs to overcome pneumonia, I needed the breath of God to help me overcome the depression of my spirit.

I don't know when I became aware of that depression. In the first few weeks of my recovery, I was in such constant physical pain I couldn't hold any thoughts in my mind for more than a second or two.

I also battled a lot of anger during those first weeks. I wasn't angry with God, though I often wondered why God had sent me back to earth and why I had to go through such intense physical agony. But even being in pain was not the issue for me. From my first day in the hospital, pain has always been present. Like many others, I've learned to live with that reality. My struggle is that I had experienced the glory and majesty of heaven only to return to earth. In my weaker moments, I didn't understand why God would return me to earth in such awful condition. Many live in greater pain, but few—if any—have experienced heaven.

Instead, my anger focused primarily on the medical staff. I suppose it was because they were there all the time. Deep inside, I seethed with an inner rage, perhaps at myself as much as the medical staff. Why wasn't I recuperating faster? I blamed them for the slowness of my recovery. In my rational moments, I knew they did the best they could. Despite my antagonism and irritation—which I'm sure they sensed—they stayed right with me and constantly encouraged me.

I didn't want encouragement—I wanted results. I wanted to be healthy again. Why couldn't my life be the way it used to be? I wanted to walk by myself, and I didn't want to depend on others all the time.

The medical staff wouldn't give me any definite answers, and that sent fresh waves of rage through my system. In retrospect,

I'm sure they told me what they could, but I was anything but a typical case. No one knew my prognosis. In fact, for several weeks, they weren't even sure if I would live, let alone make a significant recovery.

I became paranoid—I knew I wasn't rational even when I complained and demanded more attention or additional medication to alleviate the pain. Nothing suited me. The pace was too slow. They made me wait too long before responding to my bell. No one wanted to answer questions.

"How long will I have to wear this Ilizarov frame?" I asked almost every medical person who came into my room.

"I don't know," was the most common answer.

"But I want to know something," I finally said.

"A long time, a very long time," was the only other answer a nurse or doctor would give me.

A couple of times I just had to have an answer, so I kept pressing the doctor.

"Weeks. Months," he said. "We can't tell you because we don't know. If I knew, I'd tell you."

Common sense said they were doing their best, but in those days, I didn't have much common sense. Part of it was the pain, and perhaps the mammoth doses of medications affected me as well, but I wasn't a good patient. Instead of being satisfied, I kept asking myself, *Why won't they tell me? What do they know that they're hiding? There are things they're not telling me, and I have a right to know what's going on.*

During many sleepless nights, I would lie in bed, convinced that the nurses conspired against me. It never occurred to me to wonder why they would want to do that.

Then why don't they tell me anything? I'd rail as I lay there. *What can they possibly do that will hurt more than this?*

The answer was *nothing*. I endured additional pain that resulted not from the accident itself but from the process of healing. For instance, when they harvested bones out of my right hip and put them in my left arm, they made an incision six inches long—and closed it up with metal staples. When the day came for them to take out the staples, they pulled them out of my skin. As they pulled each one, I winced in pain and steeled myself so that I wouldn't scream at the top of my lungs. I couldn't remember hurting that excruciatingly. I had, of course, but I had forgotten how much torture my body could take.

The poor nurse who was extracting the staples stopped after each one. Sadness filled her eyes, and I knew she sensed how deeply the procedure hurt me. She was a large woman and always treated me as gently as she could. "I'm so sorry, Reverend," she said softly.

"I know," I mumbled. "You can't help it." Momentarily, I lapsed into my pastoral role of trying to console her. I didn't want her to feel bad for the torture I felt.

"Reverend, why don't you just haul off and yell?"

"It wouldn't do any good."

"If it was me, I'd be yelling."

"Yeah, I bet you would." I offered a faint sense of humor. "And you'd wake up every patient in the hospital."

I just never could yell voluntarily. Maybe it was a fear of losing control. Perhaps I feared that if I did scream, she and others would consider me as weak. I'm not sure of the reasons, even now. I know only that I couldn't scream like others on my floor. From several other rooms, every day I heard patients scream out in agony. I just couldn't let go like that. Instead, I'd hold my breath and sometimes break out in a cold sweat, but I wouldn't scream purposely.

Though I know I wasn't the easiest of patients in demeanor or medical requirements, the nurses of the orthopedic floor treated me with kindness and much compassion. I learned to care a great deal for them and admire their dedication. I guess they must have seen something in me as well. I know the nursing staff often bent the rules when well-wishers showed up to see me, no matter what time of day or night they came. But the sweetest moment came when I was discharged from my 105-day stay at St. Luke's. Apparently, arrangements were made with nursing staffs of other hospital floors to cover for them as the nurses from my floor all accompanied me down the elevator and to my waiting ambulance on the day of my discharge. Being surrounded by nurses that fed me, medicated me, bathed me, and did only the Lord knows what else, made my going home that day so wonderful. It was as if they were saying, "We've done our best. Now you've got to get better and come back and see us." I can only imagine how different I must have seemed to them that going-home day from the day I had arrived wavering between life and death.

In spite of my stubborn resistance to showing emotion, before I left St. Luke's, the months of intense pain finally crumbled my resolve. I broke down and cried. I felt worthless, beaten down, and useless. I was convinced I would never get any better.

"God, God, why is it like this? Why am I going through this constant pain that never seems to get any better?" Again I prayed for God to take me. I didn't want to live any longer. I wanted to go back home, and now for me, home meant heaven.

I prayed that way for days, and usually, I'd fall asleep from exhaustion. When I'd awaken, a cloak of hopelessness would spread over me again. Nothing helped.

Just before the accident, I had ordered several cassette tapes of popular Christian songs originally recorded during the 1960s and '70s by people like the Imperials and David Meece. Eva had brought them to the hospital along with a tape player, but I had no interest in listening to them.

Instead, I watched TV. I once told a friend, "I've watched every *Brady Bunch* episode at least eight times, and I know all of the dialogue by heart."

One morning between three and five o'clock, I couldn't bear to watch another TV rerun, so I decided to play the cassettes. A nurse came in and helped me set up the first cassette to play.

The first song had been recorded by the Imperials, and it was called "Praise the Lord." The lyrics suggest that when we're up against a struggle and we think we can't go on, we need to praise God. As preposterous as that prospect seemed at three o'clock in the morning in a hospital bed, I continued to listen for any help to bring me out of my deep heartache. There was a phrase in the next verse about the chains that seem to bind us falling away when we turn ourselves over to praise. The whole song centered on praising God in spite of our circumstances.

The instant the Imperials sang the second chorus about the chains, I looked down at my chains—pounds of stainless steel encasing my arm and leg. Before my accident, I'm sure I'd heard and sung that song hundreds of times. I had even played it myself. Just then, those words became a message from God—a direct hit from on high.

Before they had finished singing the song, I lay there and heard my own voice say, "Praise the Lord!"

No sooner had that song ended than David Meece sang, "We Are the Reason." His words reminded me that we are the reason Jesus Christ wept, suffered, and died on the cross. Meece sang about how he finally found that the real purpose in living was in giving every part of his life to Christ. That wasn't a new song to me, but something happened during those predawn hours. Other than music, I heard nothing else—no moaning from other rooms or footsteps of nurses in the hallway. I felt totally isolated from the world around me.

Then the dam broke. Tears slid down my cheeks, and I couldn't wipe them away—and I didn't even want to try. They just flowed. The tears wouldn't stop, and I cried as I had never wept before. I'm not sure, but I think the crying lasted for about an hour.

Slowly the sobbing subsided. Calmness swept over me, and I lay relaxed and very much at peace. That's when I realized another miracle had taken place: My depression had lifted. Vanished.

I had been healed. Again.

Stark reminders from some simple songs had changed me. The Imperials reminded me that Satan is a liar. He wants to steal our joy and replace it with hopelessness. When we're up against a struggle and we think we can't keep going, we can change that by praising God. Our chains will fall from us.

Meece encouraged me by reminding me of the real reason we have for fully living this life. It's to give everything we have to God—even the heartbreaks and pain. God is our reason to live.

That morning I determined to get on with living the rest of my life, no matter what. I made that decision with no psychiatric help, no drugs, and no counseling. As I listened to those two songs, God had healed me. The despair lifted. My mental chains had broken. I also knew that nothing I had gone through—or would endure—was as horrific as what Jesus suffered.

I'm not trying to imply that I'm against psychological help. Before and since my accident, I've sent many people for counseling. But because I wasn't open to help of any kind, God healed me in a dramatic and unexplainable way.

As I lay there, my attitude changed. I had no idea when my physical pain would end or how long I'd have to wear the Ilizarov frame, but I knew Jesus Christ was with me. I still didn't understand why God had sent me back to live with all of this agony, but that no longer mattered.

Now I was free. He had healed my mind. My body would mend slowly, but I had experienced the major victory. Never again would depression afflict me. It was just one more miracle from heaven.

11

BACK TO CHURCH

So humble yourselves under the mighty power of God, and in his good time he will honor you. Give all your worries and cares to God, for he cares about what happens to you.

1 Peter 5:6–7

Some people who have known me for a long time see me as some kind of courageous figure. I certainly haven't seen myself that way—not for an instant—because I know too much about the real me. I also know how little I did to get through my ordeal.

Despite my own perceptions, friends and church members say they received encouragement by watching me as I progressed from a totally helpless state and gradually moved toward a fairly normal lifestyle. A number of individuals have said to me in the midst of their own difficult times, "If you could go through all you endured, I can go through this."

I'm glad they've been heartened by my example, but I've had a great deal of difficulty accepting myself as a source of inspiration and courage. I don't know how to cope with their admiration and praise, because I didn't do anything. I wanted to die. How uplifting can that be?

When people tell me how inspiring I've been, I don't argue with them, of course, but I remember only too well the time David Gentiles told me that he and others would pray me back to health. I lived because others wouldn't let me die. Those praying friends are the ones who deserve the admiration.

Most of the time when people have that if-you-can-do-it attitude, I nod, acknowledge what they're saying, and add, "I'm just doing the best I can." And really, that's all I did during the worst days. Sometimes "the best I can" was nothing but to endure. Even when I struggled with depression, it was still the best I could do. Maybe that's what God honors. I don't know.

By nature, I'm a determined individual, which I admit can sometimes be a first cousin to stubbornness. Yet many times I felt terribly alone and was convinced that no one else understood. And I still think that's true. When our pain becomes intense and endures for weeks without relief, no one else really knows. I'm not sure it's worthwhile for them to know what it's like.

They care. That's what I think is important.

———

After I came home from the hospital in the middle of May, I still had to sleep in a hospital bed until February 1990—a total of thirteen months. Even after sleeping in my own house, I had setbacks of various kinds or developed infections. Back to the hospital I'd go, and some of those trips, especially in the early days, were for life-threatening infections. Sometimes I stayed two weeks and other times three. On most occasions Eva drove me there, but I always came home in an ambulance.

After they initially released me from the hospital, church members kept telling me how good I looked "considering all that's happened." No one actually said the words, but I imagined them saying, "We prayed for Don. We can't believe how well it turned out. We asked for him to live, and we asked for him to be better." That is, I was a pitiful mess, but I was alive and that's what they had asked for.

My twin sons, Joe and Christopher, were only eight at the time of the accident, and our daughter, Nicole, was thirteen. One of the things that hurt me most during my recovery was the sense of pain my children had to cope with. They didn't say a great deal, but I knew how they felt.

This is a handmade card from my son Joe, written to me in February 1989, while he was living with his grandparents. (I didn't correct the spelling.)

hi dad,
 You are the best. I love you and I hope you like the cards.
I whish this never hapined
 I love you Dad,

Joe

Months later when I finally came home, most afternoons, Joe's twin, Chris, came in from school and into the large living room where my bed was. Without saying a word, Chris would walk over and lay his head on my chest. I don't know how long his head lay there, probably not more than a full minute.

He never said a word.

He didn't need to. That simple gesture was enough. I felt so loved by my son.

After a minute or so, Chris would go into his room, get out of his school clothes, change into his play clothes, and then go outside and play. That's the way he greeted me almost every day.

I know it was hard on him—really hard on him—and he expressed his grief in the only way he knew how.

—

Just six months after the accident, I was able to participate in a very special moment for Nicole.

Southern Baptists have mission organizations for young people. The most well-known are the Royal Ambassadors for boys and Girls in Action (GAs) and Acteens for girls. As soon as she was old enough, Nicole participated in GAs and Acteens. She fulfilled all the requirements, such as Scripture memorization, various service projects, and mission trips. When she was fourteen, she learned she would be awarded the honor of Queen with Scepter at a coronation ceremony at South Park Baptist Church in June 1989.

This award is the pinnacle of Acteen participation and is presented during a church ceremony. Her receiving the award was a tribute to her own utter determination. During the time she threw herself into those activities, she wasn't able to live at home. Our friends Suzan and Stan Mauldin had opened their home to her, and she lived with them. Nicole received no emotional or physical support from me, because I was barely surviving in the hospital. She received little support from her mother, because Eva's life consisted of leaving school every afternoon and rushing to the hospital, where she stayed with me until she went home to bed.

The challenges made us all the more proud of Nicole.

One of the traditions associated with the coronation is that fathers escort their daughters down the aisle. Brothers, if the girls have any, follow and carry the crown and scepter.

Because of the timing of South Park's annual coronation, there was great doubt about my being able to be present, much less escort her down the aisle.

I'm grateful that my doctors discharged me from the hospital in time to be present for the coronation. I really wanted to be there. This wasn't her wedding, but it was the biggest thing so far in her young life, and I wanted to share the moment with her.

I was in a wheelchair, and Nicole held my arm as I rolled down the aisle. Chris and Joe walked behind us, carrying her crown and scepter on pillows. They also helped roll my chair down the aisle. I wore a suit coat and tie (my first time since the accident) along with my warm-ups split down the sides to allow for my Ilizarov.

Not only was Nicole absolutely elated that her daddy could be present for her extremely important occasion, she was thrilled that her father could "walk" her down the aisle.

Tears filled my eyes as I maneuvered down the aisle. I heard others sniffling. But I also knew that we wept tears of joy over this wonderful moment in Nicole's life.

The doctors sent me home initially, I believe, because they thought I'd recover faster in an environment with family around me. It may also have cost a lot less for me to be home. I'm not sure, but I was glad to be out of the hospital. Insurance didn't pay for any of my treatment. The bill was covered at first by workmen's compensation, and ultimately the State of Texas, because a federal court found them at fault.

Still, being in my own home wasn't much easier for me or my family, especially Eva. Every day someone had to give me shots. I had to have physical therapy treatments—all done to me and for me at home. Our living room looked like a hospital room. I did feel better being out of that sterile environment. Just being around familiar things lifted my spirit. I enjoyed being able to look out the window at my neighborhood or having people drop in to see me who didn't wear white uniforms.

The medical team sent my bed and a trapeze contraption—just like what I had used at the hospital. Nurses visited every day; physical therapists came every other day.

Some of the sweetest memories I have are of the kind people who simply spent each day with me while Eva went back to work. When church members heard that she had to return to teaching or lose her job, they decided to do what they could.

Ginny Foster, the senior pastor's wife, organized a group of people to stay with me each day. Ginny organized what she laughingly called the "Don Patrol"—mostly women from the church, along with a few retired men.

It was about seven hours from the time Eva left in the morning until she returned. My sleep habits depended on when I could fight the pain no more and would pass out. But gradually, a pattern began to emerge. I would generally go to sleep about two or three o'clock in the morning and wake up around ten. The Don Patrol arrived about nine o'clock while I was still asleep. They either prepared lunch for me or brought it with them.

Often I would awake to find a charming woman knitting at the end of my bed. Or perhaps an older man would be reading the *Houston Chronicle*. He'd lower the newspaper and grin at me, "Good morning. Do you need anything?"

The parade of sweet faces changed every day. Although the volunteers were different, the goals remained the same: Take care of Don and keep him company.

As I lay in bed day after day, I realized how much others had done for us. While I was still hospitalized, friends from the Alvin church had packed up our furniture and moved us to a new house, where I could be on the ground level with no stairs to worry about.

During the day, I would look through the patio window from my "hospital room." Often I spotted high schoolers Brandon and Matt Mealer and their buddy Chris Alston mowing our lawn.

Chris arranged to borrow our van one night and surprise me by taking me to a movie. I don't even remember what the movie was, but I will never forget his thoughtfulness. Once when our fence blew down during a windstorm, it was back up before we could call anyone to help. Only God knows all the kindnesses shown to us during my recovery.

———

As I began to stir in my bed each morning, my "keeper" would get up and bring me a toothbrush and a pan to brush my teeth and wash my face. I'd have a glass of juice held to my lips and later a huge lunch ready for me.

After feeding me, washing up, and making sure I was as comfortable as my physical condition would allow, they all asked the same question: "Is there anything else I can get for you before I leave?"

My answer was always the same: "No, thanks." I would muster what I hoped was my best smile. It probably wasn't, but they always smiled back.

"It's all right. I'll be fine."

The capacity for sacrifice and service that human beings have for one another knows no bounds. With all our faults, surely God must have meant that the kindnesses shown to me during my injury and recovery were paramount examples of us being created in his image.

Within an hour or so after my daily Don Patrol angel quietly exited, the door would open, and Eva would enter from a long day at school. She always gave me a big smile and kissed me.

"Are you all right?" she would ask.

"I'm fine," I would say, meaning it.

I couldn't put my feelings into words then, but the assurance that I had been visited by an angel from the Don Patrol caused my spirit to soar.

For months after I came home, good-hearted members of the Don Patrol transported me back and forth for water therapy, which was done near our home in Alvin. During the first thirteen months, if I wasn't inside the hospital, I was lying in the hospital bed at the house. For months, I probably wasn't out of the bed more than five minutes a day except for therapy. Some days I didn't even get out of bed.

The worst part is that once I was in the hospital bed, I was completely incapacitated. I couldn't get up or do anything for myself. Without the help of the therapist, I never would have sat up or been able to move on my own again.

Slowly, gradually, I learned to walk again. The first day I got out of bed on my own, I took three steps. I slumped back onto the bed, feeling a wave of exhaustion overwhelm me. But I smiled. *I had walked.* Three steps sounds like so little, and yet I felt a powerful sense of accomplishment.

So much of recovery from a trauma of this magnitude has a striking similarity to training a child in infancy. I had been helpless for such a long time that when I could finally go to the bathroom by myself, it felt like a remarkable accomplishment. Walking again was a stark reminder of what we all take for granted every day as we talk, move, and live.

When I could walk again, it was not only a singular accomplishment but a tribute to hundreds of medical people who worked tirelessly to help me. It was also a tribute to my friends and family who believed in me, although they couldn't have known just how difficult it would be for me to put one foot in front of the other.

While I suppose walking represented a certain triumph of will, it also meant I could begin to live in relative normalcy. I often thought of the last night at Trinity Pines when J. V. Thomas and I took our walk around the camp. That was my last normal walk ever. For many months no one was sure I'd ever walk again. For a long time, taking just three shaky steps seemed like climbing Mount Everest.

"I did it!" I shouted to the silent room. "I walked! I walked."

Taking those first steps at home on my own remains one of the best moments of my recovery. Those few steps convinced me that I was getting better. Now I had goals to work toward. I had gone through the worst part of the recovery. I knew I would continue to improve. Each day I took a few more steps. By the end of the week, I had made a complete circle of the living room.

When Eva came home and watched me demonstrate my daily progress, her smile made me feel as if I had won a marathon. She reacted with absolute joyful delight the afternoon I showed her that I could walk throughout the house all by myself.

A week after I came home from the hospital, I had decided I wanted to go to church on a Sunday morning.

In retrospect, it was premature, but I felt a burning desire to be back with people I loved and to worship with them. With the help of a small group, we planned for them to help me get there. In case I couldn't make it, we didn't want to disappoint anyone, so we decided not to announce it to the congregation.

By then I could sit in a wheelchair—as long as someone was there to lift me out of bed and into it—but I still couldn't stand up. Six friends from church came to our house and took the seats out of one of the church vans. At the church, they had constructed a ramp so they could roll me up to its doors.

I kept thinking of all the work I had laid on them, and several times I started to apologize, but they assured me it was their pleasure.

Then I remembered Jay's words. My family and friends saw me the first day of the accident. I never saw what I looked like.

They endured the shock and the fear. They had to come to grips with the possibility of my death or my long-term disability. In some respects, this ordeal was more difficult for my family and friends than it was for me. They loved being able to help me. In a way, this was part of their own recovery, and they were glad to be able to do something special for me.

Yet, as much as I wanted to attend the worship service that morning, it was still hard to let them do everything for me. I felt totally helpless and absolutely dependent on them. As I realized that once again, I smiled.

"Thank you," I said and then allowed them to take care of me.

They carefully put me into the van, drove me to the church, and pulled up at the side door. When one of the men in the van opened the door, church members on their way into the sanctuary saw me.

"Look! It's Pastor Don!" someone yelled.

I heard cheering and clapping as people stood around and made way for the men to wheel me up the ramp.

Just then, everything turned chaotic. People rushed toward me. Several cheered. It seemed as if everyone wanted to touch me or shake my hand. I could hardly believe the fuss they made over me.

Finally someone wheeled me inside and stopped my chair in front of the platform near the church organ. It wasn't possible to lift me up.

By then the entire congregation had become aware that I was in front of the sanctuary. I smiled as I thought, *It's only taken me five months to get from the conference at Trinity Pines back to church. I may be slow, but I'm faithful.*

Just then someone whispered in my ear, "We want you to say something to the congregation." He got behind me and steered me toward the center of the sanctuary, right in front of the pulpit.

By then exhaustion had begun to seep in. It had probably nagged at me all along, but I had been so determined to get back to church, I refused to admit how tired I felt. I had been out of bed more than two hours. That was the longest time I had been out of bed up to that point, and also the longest time I had spent in a wheelchair.

In that moment, I realized I had been foolish in wanting to come, because I wasn't up to the physical demands on my body. My stubbornness had overestimated my endurance.

Perhaps just as bad, I became completely overwhelmed at the congregation's loving response. I didn't know if I could speak. What could I say after all those weeks of absence and all I'd been through?

While I was still trying to figure that out, someone thrust a microphone in my hand. As I clutched it, I kept thinking, *You people really have no idea how little I contributed to my recovery. You see it as a triumph. I see it merely as survival.*

Just then spontaneous applause broke out. I had expected them to be glad to see me; I had not been prepared for the avalanche of praise to God. Every person in that building stood, and the applause began—and it kept on for a long time. I finally waved them to stop.

As I stared at them, I felt guilty about their applause and excitement. I couldn't believe those people were applauding me. *If they only knew,* I thought. *If they only knew.*

Then God spoke to me. This was one of the few times in my life when I heard a very clear voice inside my head.

They're not applauding for you.

Just those words, but it made a difference and I could speak. Finally, I had it straight. They were giving thanks to God for what he had done for me. God had brought me back from death to life once again. I relaxed. This was a moment to glorify God. This wasn't praise for me.

I still had to wait for what seemed like a long time until the applause ceased. I spoke only four words. Anyone who was there that glorious day can tell you what they were: "You prayed. I'm here."

The congregation erupted in spontaneous applause again. If I had said anything else, I'm sure they wouldn't have heard it anyway.

I couldn't say it, but I believed then—and still do—that I survived only because a number of people wanted me to. They were relentless, passionate, and desperate, and they believed God would hear them. People prayed for me who had never seriously prayed before; some who hadn't uttered a word of petition in years cried out to God to spare me. My experience brought people to their knees, and many of them had changed in the process of praying for me to live.

When I did live, those same people—especially those who hadn't been in the habit of praying—said the experience revolutionized their lives. In some instances, individuals I had never met—from Cottonwood, Arizona, to Buffalo, New York—heard my story second-, third-, and fourthhand. Over the next three years, people would approach me and say, "I saw you on a video interview. You're the man! I prayed for you." Or they heard one of the audiotapes of my testimony distributed by my church and would say, "You just don't know what it means. God heard *our* prayers, and we're so happy you lived."

To some individuals, I'm not really a person but a symbol. For them, I represent answered prayer. They may remember my ministry at South Park Church or even some of the messages I preached, but what they remember most is that they sought God's face in deep, sincere, earnest prayer. They pleaded for me to survive, and I did. I don't know what to make of it, except to say that this is something outside of and beyond me.

I think I'm also a human response to some of the questions people wanted answered. Since I began to tell others about my

Don with sons Joe and Chris in 1982.

Don's Ford Escort after the accident. The roof was removed to extract Don and was laid back on top after the car arrived at the wrecking yard.

The accident scene.

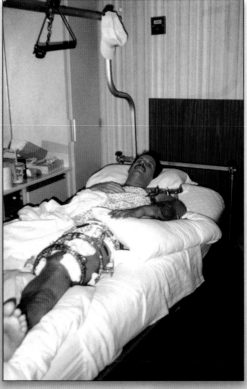

Don wearing the Ilizarov bone growth device.

Don attends Nicole's Girls in Action coronation.

Chris and Don, near the crest of Mt. McKinley, Denali, Alaska.
Don preached at the base of the mountain near Willow.

Don on the set of *700 Club*.

Don receives a gift from a chairwoman of the Pueblo
Navajo tribe, after he addressed their gathering.

Don stands at the Holocaust Memorial in Berlin
after preaching near the site of the Berlin Wall.

Don speaks in Puerto Rico
(translator Ricky Feliciano of Pura Vida).

People come forward following
Don's testimony in Puerto Rico.

Don preaches in Sweden during one of his four speaking
tours of the country (translator Joel Sjoberg).

Don signs books at a church in Germany that had been turned into a museum during its days behind the Iron Curtain. As a rule Europeans don't queue up, they just come.

Don stands by a sign after leaving Ft. Peck. Note the necklace given to Don by a young Native American after Don prayed for him. This is a great honor.

Don preaches to 100,000 at Lifelight Festival
in South Dakota.

Don with Pat Boone.

experience in heaven, I can't begin to count the people who have come to me and asked such questions as, Is heaven real? What is heaven really like? Or they'll ask specific questions about the praise or the streets of gold. Someone seems to always mention a recently departed loved one.

Just to know that I've been there and come back to earth and am able to talk to them seems to bring deep comfort to many. Sometimes it amazes me.

Others look at the marks on my body even today and say, "You're a miracle because of all you went through. You're a walking miracle."

12

OPENING UP

For we know that when this earthly tent we live in is taken down—when we die and leave these bodies—we will have a home in heaven, an eternal body made for us by God himself and not by human hands. We grow weary in our present bodies, and we long for the day when we will put on our heavenly bodies like new clothing. For we will not be spirits without bodies, but we will put on new heavenly bodies. Our dying bodies make us groan and sigh, but it's not that we want to die and have no bodies at all. We want to slip into our new bodies so that these dying bodies will be swallowed up by everlasting life.

2 Corinthians 5:1–4

God used my closest friend, David Gentiles, to keep me alive, and I'm grateful. He also used David again in my life nearly two years after the accident.

Until then I had never talked to anyone about my heavenly experience. In a general sense, I had talked to Eva, but I always closed off the conversation before she asked questions. She tacitly understood that part of my experience was off-limits. To her credit, she never pressured me to say anything more.

It wasn't that I wanted to withhold anything from Eva; I just couldn't talk about the experience. At times I felt that it had been too sacred and that to try to explain it would diminish the incident.

Nearly a year and a half after my release from the hospital, David came to the Houston area for a discipleship weekend. He used that as an excuse to come to the house and spend time with me.

When the two of us were alone, I had a flashback to the time when I had been lying in ICU and had told him that I couldn't go on. That's when he had told me that he would pray me through. We talked about that day, and I thanked him again for his friendship and relentless commitment to prayer.

"How are you feeling now?" he asked.

"I'm in pain." I tried to laugh and added, "I'm always in pain, but that's not the worst part for me right now."

He leaned closer. "What is the worst part?"

"I just don't know where I'm going. I lack any clear direction about my future."

David listened as I talked about the things I would like to do, the things I couldn't physically do, and how I wasn't sure that God wanted me to continue at South Park. I felt loved and needed there, but I wasn't sure that was where I should be.

He listened for a long time and then asked gently, "What did you learn from your accident and recovery experience?"

For three or four minutes I shared several things, especially about letting other people inside and allowing them to help me. Then I said, "But in the midst of all this suffering and despondency, I have learned that heaven is real."

He raised his eyebrows. "What do you mean by that?"

Slowly, hesitantly, I shared a little—very little—about my brief visit to heaven. "Tell me more," he said, and I didn't hear it as prying. He was my friend and wanted to know. I also sensed that I could speak about heaven to David and that, as much as any human being was able, he would understand.

"I died in that accident. The next moment I stood in heaven," I said.

He leaned forward, and although he waited silently for me to continue, I saw the excitement in his eyes.

The more I shared, the more animated he became. In retrospect, I believe David's exuberance was a combination of my personal confirmation of heaven's reality and his relief in knowing something good had come out of my long nightmare.

After I had shared my experience in heaven, he said nothing, and a peaceful silence filled the room. Our friendship was such that we didn't have to fill the gap with words.

David finally nodded slowly and asked, "Why haven't you talked about this before?"

"I have two very good reasons. Number one, if I go around talking about having been in heaven, people will think I'm nuts."

"Why would you think that? I heard you, and I didn't—"

"Number two," I said, interrupting him, "I don't want to go over that experience again. It's . . . well, it's just too personal. Too special. This is something I haven't even processed enough to understand it myself. It's not that I don't want to share it, but I don't think I can."

"Why do you think you experienced heaven if you're not supposed to share it?"

"I don't have an answer for that question."

"Why?"

"I'll tell you a better question I've asked myself—Why did I experience it and have it taken away from me? What was that all about?" Months of pent-up anger burst forth, and all the interior pain spewed out. "Okay, why did I have to go through this? I saw the glory and the beauty—the most powerful, overwhelming experiences in my life—and then I had to come back. Why? For this?" I pointed to my arm and leg. "Listen. I was in an accident that took my life. Immediately I went to heaven, and it was greater and more wonderful than anything I've ever imagined. I had a magnificent taste of heaven, and then I was pulled back to this life again. My body is a mess. I'm constantly in pain. I'll never be healthy or strong again. I'm still processing this because—because, frankly it all seems cruel to me."

David stared at me and asked again, "Why do you think you experienced it if you're not supposed to share it?"

"Like I said, I don't have an answer for that question."

"Is it possible that God took you to heaven and brought you back for you to share what happened to you? Don't you realize what a powerful encouragement you can be to others?"

His words shocked me. I had been so focused on myself, I hadn't thought about anyone else.

I broke down as I tried to relate to him how I felt and to explain it to myself. I cried in his presence, and I knew it was all right.

For perhaps twenty minutes we discussed it. David nudged me, and although I knew he was right, it still wasn't easy for me to share my experience.

Finally David said, "I want you to make a covenant with me."

"What kind of covenant?"

"Simple. Pick two people you trust. Just tell them a little of your experience and gauge their response." He went on to explain that if they thought I was crazy or that I had hallucinated, then I would never have to speak about it again.

"But if they rejoice with you," he said, "and if they urge you to tell them more, I want you to take this as a sign—a sign that God wants you to talk about those ninety minutes you spent in heaven."

After considering the matter carefully, I covenanted with him. "I can do that much."

"When?"

"I promise to do it soon."

"Very soon, right?"

"Okay, I promise I won't put it off."

David prayed for me, and as I listened to him speak, the certainty came over me. It was no longer a choice—I had to speak out—but I would do it my way.

First, I decided on those I could trust with my holy secret. Once I had narrowed it down to a handful, I still took a cautious approach. I made sure it was a one-to-one conversation. I'd wait until the matter of my health came up—and it always did—and then I'd say something simple such as, "You know, I died that day. And I woke up in heaven."

The reaction was the same each time: "Tell me more." They didn't always say those words, but that's what they wanted. I could see their eyes widen, and they wanted to know more.

As I shared a little more, no one questioned my sanity. No one told me I had hallucinated.

"You have to tell people about this," one of them said.

"That experience wasn't just for you," another friend said. "It's for us as well. It's for me."

As I listened to each one over the next two weeks, I realized I was right back where I had been in the hospital the time Jay had rebuked me. That time I wouldn't let anyone help me, and it was selfish. This time I wouldn't share what had happened to me—and it was also selfish.

"Okay, I'll talk about it," I vowed to myself.

Since virtually everyone already knew about my tragic auto accident, I used the occasion as the natural catalyst to speak about my time in heaven—cautiously at first. As people responded with overwhelming support, I became more open and less careful about the people with whom I shared my story.

I want to make it clear that even though I knew it was what I was supposed to do, it wasn't easy for me. Even now, years later, it's just against my nature to talk deeply and personally about things in my life. Today, I only discuss my glimpse of heaven when someone asks, and then only because I feel that person really wants to know. Otherwise, I still wouldn't talk about it.

That's part of the reason it's taken me so many years to write this book. I didn't want my experience in heaven and my return to earth to be my sole reason for being alive. On the contrary, it was such an extraordinarily personal and intimate experience that going back over it repeatedly isn't something I feel comfortable doing.

I talk about my experience both publicly and to individuals. I'm writing about what happened because my story seems to mean so much to people for many different reasons. For example, when I speak to any large crowd, at least one person will be present who has recently lost a loved one and needs assurance of that person's destination.

When I finish speaking, it still amazes me to see how quickly the line forms of those who want to talk to me. They come with tears in their eyes and grief written all over their faces. I feel so grateful that I can offer them peace and assurance.

I've accepted that my words do bring comfort, but it was never something I thought about doing. If it hadn't been for David Gentiles pushing me, I'm sure that even to this day I wouldn't have told anyone.

I'm also grateful for his urging me, because I've seen the effect not only in worship services but also when I've conducted funerals. In fact, my experience has changed many things about the way I look at life. I've changed the way I do funerals. Now I can speak authoritatively about heaven from firsthand knowledge.

Besides my own miraculous experience, four things stand out from my heavenly journey. First, I'm thoroughly convinced that God answers prayer. Answered prayer is why I'm still alive. Second, I have an unquestionable belief that God still is in the miracle business. Too many people read about the supernatural in the Bible and think, *That's the way it was in biblical times.* I'm convinced that God continues to do the more-than-ordinary. Every day I thank God that I'm a living, walking, talking miracle.

Third, I want as many people as possible to go to heaven. I've always believed Christian theology that declares heaven is real and a place for God's people. Since my own experience of having been there, I've felt a stronger sense of responsibility to make the way absolutely clear. Not only do I want people to go to heaven, I now feel an urgency about helping them open their lives so they can be assured that's where they'll go when they die.

I've actually thought about the people who get killed on the highways. In evangelistic services, some have used such stories as a scare tactic to manipulate people into making commitments to Jesus Christ. But because of my experience, I see such accidents as definite possibilities of death at any moment in our lives. I don't want to see others die without Jesus Christ.

Finally, one time, Dick Onerecker and I talked about this urgency. He understood why I felt that way. Then I told him, "Again, Dick, I want to thank you for saving my life. I obviously can't thank you enough for your faithfulness in obeying God that rainy day."

"It was what anybody would have done," he said, and then he started crying.

"I didn't mean to upset you," I said, feeling bad that I had said something to make him cry like that. "That's the last thing on earth I'd ever want to do."

"That's not what I'm crying about."

Several minutes lapsed before he finally pulled himself back together again.

"What were you crying about?" I asked.

"I was thinking that I came upon the scene of the accident and I asked the officer if I could pray for you—and I thought of it as just something any Christian would do. Although he said you were dead, I knew—I just knew—I had to pray for you. I could only think that you were hurt, and I wanted to make you feel better. I didn't do anything unusual."

"But you did. When the officer told you I was already dead—"

"Listen to me, Don. If you saw a little kid run out in the street, you'd dash out there and try to save the child's life. Human nature is like that. We try to preserve life, and I will do that any time I get the opportunity. So would you."

We were sitting in a restaurant, and he paused to look around. "Yet here we are sitting in this place, surrounded by people, many of whom are probably lost and going to hell, and we won't say a word about how they can have eternal life. Something is wrong with us."

"You're absolutely right," I said. "We're willing to save someone in a visible crisis, but a lot of folks are in spiritual crisis and we don't say a word about how they can get out of it."

"That's why I was crying. I've been convicted about my silence, my fear of speaking to people, my reluctance to speak up."

Dick said then, and again later, that hearing my experience and his role in my coming back to earth had set him free. After that he felt a boldness to talk about Jesus Christ that he hadn't had before.

13

THE CLASPING HAND

He is your God, the one who is worthy of your praise, the one who has done mighty miracles that you yourself have seen.

Deuteronomy 10:21

I was privileged to share my story in Dick's church, Klein First Baptist, a little more than a year after the accident. His wife, Anita, was there, and so was my own family. Because I still wore leg braces, two people had to help me walk up on the platform.

I told everyone about the accident and about Dick's part in bringing me back. "I believe I'm alive today because Dick prayed me back to earth," I said. "In my first moments of consciousness, two things stand out. First, I was singing 'What a Friend We Have in Jesus.' The second was that Dick's hand gripped mine and held it tight."

After the morning worship, many of us went out to lunch together at a Chinese restaurant. Anita sat across from me. I remember sipping my wonton soup and having a delightful time with the church members.

When there was a lull in the conversation, Anita leaned across the table and said in a low voice, "I appreciated everything you said this morning."

"Thank you—"

"There's just one thing—one thing I need to correct about what you said in your message."

"Really?" Her words shocked me. "I tried to be as accurate as possible in everything I said. I certainly didn't intend to exaggerate anything. What did I say that was incorrect?"

"You were talking about Dick getting into the car with you. Then you said he prayed for you while he was holding your hand."

"Yes, I remember that part very distinctly. I have a number of memory gaps, and most of the things I don't remember." That morning I had readily admitted that some of the information I gave came secondhand. "The one thing that's totally clear was Dick being in the car and praying with me."

"That's true. He did get in the car and pray with you." She leaned closer. "But, Don, he never held your hand."

"I distinctly remember holding his hand."

"That didn't happen. It was physically impossible."

"But I remember that so clearly. It's one of the most vivid—"

"Think about it. Dick leaned over from the rear of the trunk over the backseat and put his hand on your *shoulder* and touched you. You were facing forward and your left arm was barely hanging together."

"Yes, that's true."

"Dick said you were slumped over on the seat toward the passenger side."

I closed my eyes, visualizing what she had just said. I nodded.

"Your right hand was on the floor of the passenger side of the car. Although the tarp covered the car, there was enough light for him to see your hand down there. There was no way Dick could have reached your right hand."

"But . . . but . . ." I sputtered.

"Someone was holding your hand. But it wasn't Dick."

"If it wasn't Dick's hand, whose was it?"

She smiled and said, "I think you know."

I put down my spoon and stared at her for several seconds. I had no doubt whatsoever that someone had held my hand. Then I understood. "Yes, I think I know too."

Immediately I thought of the verse in Hebrews about entertaining angels unaware. As I pondered for a moment, I also remembered other incidents where there was nothing but a spiritual explanation. For instance, many times in the hospital room in the middle of the night, I would be at my worst. I never saw or heard anyone, but I felt a presence—something—someone—sustaining and encouraging me. That also was something I hadn't talked about. I couldn't explain it, so I assumed others wouldn't understand.

This was another miracle, and I wouldn't have known about it if Anita hadn't corrected me.

Five years after my accident, Dick and I both appeared on Pat Robertson's *700 Club*. A camera crew came to Texas to reenact the accident and then asked me to talk about my visit to heaven's gates. The *700 Club* aired that segment many times over the next two years.

In one of life's great ironic twists, Dick died of a heart attack in 2001. I confess that I was saddened to hear of his passing, but delighted that he is in glory. Dick saved my life, and God took him to heaven first. I was glad he heard me share about my journey to heaven before he made his own trip.

Since that experience with Anita a little more than a year after my accident, I've been more convinced than ever that

God brought me back to this earth for a purpose. The angel gripping my hand was God's way of sustaining me and letting me know that he would not let go of me no matter how hard things became.

I may not feel that hand each day, but I know it's there.

14

THE NEW NORMAL

"I will give you back your health and heal your wounds, says the Lord. Now you are called an outcast—'Jerusalem for whom nobody cares.'"

Jeremiah 30:17

Some things happen to us from which we never recover, and they disrupt the normalcy of our lives. That's how life is. Human nature has a tendency to try to reconstruct old ways and pick up where we left off. If we're wise, we won't continue to go back to the way things were (we can't anyway). We must instead forget the old standard and accept a "new normal."

I wasted a lot of time thinking about how I used to be healthy and had no physical limitations. In my mind, I'd reconstruct how life *ought* to be, but in reality, I knew my life would never be the same. I had to adjust and accept my physical limits as part of my new normal.

As a child I'd sit on a big brown rug in my great-grandparents' living room and listen to them talk about the good old days. After hearing several stories, I thought, *Those days weren't that good*—at least the recollections they shared didn't seem so great. Maybe for them they truly were the good old days, or perhaps they forgot the negative parts of those days. At some points in our lives, most of us want to go back to a simpler, healthier, or happier time. We can't, but we still keep dreaming about how it once was.

In my twenties, when I was a disc jockey, we used to play oldies, and people who called in to request those songs often commented that music used to be better than it is now. The reality is that in the old days we played good and bad records, but the bad ones faded quickly from memory just like bad ones do now. No one ever asked us to play the music that bombed. The good songs make the former times seem great, as if all the music was outstanding. In reality, there was bad music thirty years ago or fifty years ago—in fact, a lot of bad music. The same is true with experiences. We tend to forget the negative and go back to recapture pleasant events. The reality is, we have selectively remembered—and just as selectively forgotten.

Once that idea got through to me, I decided I couldn't recapture the past. No matter how much I tried to idealize it, that part of my life was over and I would never be healthy or strong again. The only thing for me to do was to discover a new normal.

Yes, I said to myself, *there are things I will never be able to do again. I don't like that and may even hate it, but that doesn't change the way things are. The sooner I make peace with that fact and accept the way things are, the sooner I'll be able to live in peace and enjoy my new normalcy.*

Here's an example of what I mean.

In early 2000, I took a group of college kids on a ski trip from Houston to Colorado. Skiing is one of the things I'd always loved doing. Unable to participate, I sat in a clubhouse at the bottom of the hill, gazed out the window, and watched them glide down. Sadness came over me, and I thought, *I made a big mistake. I should never have come here.* As happy as I was for them, I mourned over my inability ever to ski again.

Then I thought for the thousandth time of other things I would never do again. When I was a senior pastor, most of the adults greeted me at the door following each morning service. "Enjoyed your sermon," they'd said. "Great service."

Kids, however, behaved differently. They'd race up with a picture they'd colored for me. Before my accident, I loved the kids flocking around me; I'd kneel down and talk with them. After my recovery, I couldn't squat down and stare at their smiling faces the way I used to before as I said, "Thank you very much. I really like this picture. This is very nice."

After my accident, the best I could do was lean forward and talk to them. Perhaps that doesn't seem like a big thing, but it is for me. I'll never squat again; I'll never be able to kneel so that I can be at a child's level again, because my legs won't give me the ability to do that.

Here's another example: When I go to a drive-through fast-food restaurant, I can't reach for the change with my left arm. The best I can do is reach out across my body with my right arm. It must look strange, and I get a few odd looks, but it's the best I can do.

While neither of these examples is particularly dramatic, they are nonetheless reminders that sometimes things we take for granted every day can be taken from us permanently and suddenly, and we're changed forever.

During my long hospitalization, somebody gave me a magazine article about a young man who lost his sight. He went through an incredibly bitter, depressive time. He wrote that he got so demoralized that a friend who cared enough about him to tell him the truth said, "You just need to get past this."

I paused from reading and thought, *Yes, that sounds like the way I was after my accident.* The article went on, however, to tell the practical instructions the blind man's friend gave him: "I want you to make a list of all the stuff you can still do."

"Now what kind of a list would that be?" the angry blind man asked.

"Just do it for me. You can't write it, obviously, but you can get a tape recorder and dictate it. Just make a list of all the things you can still do. And I'm talking about simple things like 'I can still smell flowers.' Make the list as extensive as you can. When you're finished, I want to hear that list."

The blind man finally agreed and made the list. I don't know how much time passed, but when the friend returned, the blind man was smiling and peaceful.

"You seem like you're in a much better frame of mind than the last time I saw you," the friend said.

"I am. I really am, and that's because I've been working on my list."

"How many things are on your list?"

"About a thousand so far."

"That's fantastic."

"Some of them are very simple. None of them are big, but there are thousands of things I can still do."

The blind man had changed so radically that his friend asked, "Tell me what made you change."

"I've decided to do all the stuff I can. The more I thought about it, the fewer limitations I saw. There are thousands of things I can do—and I'm going to do them for the rest of my life."

After I read that article, I thought, *That's exactly what I need—not mourning, pining, and going back over the way things used to be or what I used to have that I don't have anymore. Instead, I need to discover what I have now, not only to celebrate but also to recognize I'm not helpless.*

145

As I continued to ponder that idea, I realized I had more going for me than I thought. I had focused so heavily on my losses that I had forgotten what I had left. And I hadn't realized the opportunities I might never have tried otherwise.

In the article, the blind man said something like, "I'm not going to worry about what I can't do. I'm going to do what I can do well." Those words seemed simple.

I read that article at just the right time, and the words seemed incredibly profound. God had sent the message I needed when I needed it. It was one of those powerful moments that caused me to say, "I've got to get on with my life. Whatever I have, I'm going to use it and magnify it to the max."

I'm running out of time, I thought, *but so is everyone else.* I suppose I'm more conscious of time than some people are for two reasons: First, I lost a big chunk of my life because of the accident. Second, I know we don't get to stay long on this earth. As many of the old hymns say, we're really like strangers passing through. It's something we all know from reading the Bible and other books, but those realizations became a wake-up call for me.

I also know that my loved ones are waiting for me at the gate. Some days I can't wait to get back there.

I also realize that I have to wait until God sends me back.

———

Members of South Park Baptist Church moved our family while I was hospitalized. We had been living in a town called Friendswood, about ten miles from the church. We had needed a place nearer the church but hadn't found one. While I was in the hospital, the church leaders found a house, rented it, packed up everything for us, and moved us. When I got out of the hospital, I entered a house I had never seen before. After the ambulance backed up and unloaded me from a gurney to my home hospital bed, I stared at our house for the first time.

I soon adjusted to the new living quarters, because for a long time I could only see the living room, where they set up my hospital bed.

In some ways the move into the rented house was more difficult on the family than on me. I sensed some of the adjustments and difficulties my wife went through with my illness. Eva almost lost her job because she had spent so much time with me that she ran out of conference days, vacation days, and sick days. Other teachers donated their own sick days to her so she could come and be with me in the hospital. Eventually, she ran out of those donated days and had to go back to work. She was our primary source of income.

Eva's colleagues at Robert Louis Stevenson Primary School in Alvin often graded her papers for her, wrote her lesson plans, and covered her classes when she left early to come see me in the hospital. Her fellow teachers even made little gifts to give our kids each day so they would have something to look forward to. They called them "surprise boxes." Fellow teachers also came to our home, along with church members, to clean our house and bring meals. Had it not been for the teachers and the church, Eva would have certainly lost her job and so would I. Yet even with all these incredibly sacrificial gifts and assistance, how she and our children got through that spring semester of 1989 remains a miracle.

One time when Eva inquired about my long-term prognosis, a nurse told her, "Honey, you don't need to know all of that, you're just a wife."

To that nurse, she may have been "just a wife," but Eva took over and functioned for both of us after my accident. I had always taken care of the bills, bank accounts, insurance, and most family matters. She had no choice but to handle them herself, and she did everything well. Eva found strength and a new level of confidence. God provided her with the wisdom to help her take care of family matters. She also learned to remain calm during my complaints and grumbling throughout my lengthy recovery.

The church didn't stop paying me, but we realized that they might, and they were entitled to because I wasn't working. We never talked about the money, but it was always a possibility that hung over our heads.

When the State of Texas was found at fault for the accident, the law limited their liability to $250,000. All the money went to hospital bills, and a quarter of a million dollars didn't make much of a dent.

Ironically, the attorney general of Texas defended the man who drove the truck that hit me, because the defendant was an indigent inmate. Therefore my tax dollars went to defend the state and the man who caused the accident. Isn't life strange sometimes?

During the 105 days I spent in the hospital, Eva had the most strain. Not only did she take on the burden of everything in our home, she got up at 6:00 every morning and did everything she had to do around the house and hurried to school. As soon as school was over, she rushed to my bedside, where she stayed until 10:30 every night. Day after day was the same stressful routine.

One of the most challenging experiences for her—by herself—was to buy a van to replace my wrecked car. By then, I was home and able to walk with my Ilizarov still attached. That meant, however, that if I wanted to go anywhere, we had to have a van to transport me. We had no idea how long it would be before I could sit in a normal sedan.

Eva had never bought a vehicle in her life, but she didn't complain. She went to a dealer, test-drove a van, picked out one, and brought it home. "Here's our van," she said.

She made me proud of her—and I felt very grateful.

I learned to drive again in that van. One day as the family was washing it, I walked outside still wearing my Ilizarov. As I lumbered around the van, I noticed that the driver's side door was open. Peering inside, I calculated what it would take for me and my thirty pounds of stainless steel to get behind the wheel. While the family wasn't looking, I maneuvered myself into the seat and started the engine. My family was stunned.

Eva came around to the door and asked, "What are you doing?"

I smiled and said, "I'm going for a drive!"

Incredulous, she stammered, "But you can't."

However, something told me that not having driven for nearly a year, and having had my last drive end in my death, it was now or never for taking the wheel and driving again.

I backed out slowly and drove around the block. It wasn't a long drive, but it was another milestone in my recovery. I'm still not very fond of eighteen-wheelers or long two-lane bridges, but so far I manage to get where I'm going.

Of course, it fell on Eva to make all my appointments and to see that I got to my doctor's office twice a week. And I must add that I wasn't the easiest person to look after. In fact, I was difficult. As my health improved, I became demanding and curt (I wasn't aware of that), and Eva agonized over trying to please me, although she handled it well.

The fact is that I was very unhappy. Many of my problems stemmed from my feeling completely helpless. For a long time I couldn't even get myself a glass of water. Even if I could have poured one for myself, I couldn't have drunk it without help. Even the simplest tasks made me feel useless.

Eva often had to make decisions on the spot without talking to me. She did the best she could. At times, when Eva related what she had done, I was quick to let her know how I would have done it. Almost immediately, I'd realize I hurt her feelings when I did that, but the words had been said. I reminded myself, and her, "I'm sorry. You're doing the best you can." I also reminded myself that regardless of how I would have done things, I wasn't able to do them.

Although she said little during that period, she later allowed me to read what she wrote in her diary. One entry reads: "Don is critical of everything I do. He must be getting better."

That's both sad and funny to me. She knew I was getting better because I started to make decisions again. The desire to get active in doing things was her yardstick for my recovery. I seemed to want to get more involved in life and to question what was going on.

I just wish I had been a better patient and made it easier for her.

The worst part of my convalescence for the family was that we farmed out our three kids. They weren't orphans, but they lived with other people for about six months. Our twin sons stayed with Eva's parents in Louisiana. I know they weren't happy about having to move so far away. The distance made the boys feel detached and separated, but they handled it quite well. They were still in elementary school and, at that age, it probably wasn't too difficult relocating. Nicole, who was five years older and thirteen at the time, moved in with her girlfriend's family and was able to stay in her middle school. It would have been much more traumatic for her to move away.

The accident happened in January, and the kids didn't come home permanently until June. I felt terrible that we couldn't provide for our children.

The kids came to see me on weekends during my hospital stays, which was tough on them. When they made their first visit to the hospital, a staff psychologist did a kind thing for them.

He took all three kids into a room and showed them a life-size dummy with devices attached to it, similar to what was on my body. This way he could explain what they would see when they entered my room.

I'm glad he did that for them, because even many adults, not having that kind of preparation, showed obvious shock when they first saw me. In my condition, I interpreted their reactions as horror.

When the children came into my room the first time, all three of them stepped as close as they could to hug me. They loved me and wanted to see for themselves that I was okay. Of course, I was barely alive, but it still did me a lot of good just to see them. The staff didn't let them stay long. As awful as I looked, the children believed me when I said I would get well.

After they left, Eva came back into ICU. I don't remember this—I don't remember much from those days. She said I looked at her through my oxygen mask and said, "We have the best kids in the world."

I've never gotten the impression that our children felt as if they had missed anything, but I sometimes felt they were cheated out of experiences with their father.

When I finally was out and could walk, I remember trying to play pitch with the boys, even though I knew I couldn't take more than a step or two. If one of them hit a ball that went out of my immediate range, I couldn't chase it. They felt terrible about that.

I sensed my limitation kept them from enjoying the game, so we stopped doing it. Although they didn't say so, I knew they didn't want to see me try to run or risk falling down—though many times I did fall.

Also, both boys like to surf, and before the accident, I went surfing with them. After I was able to walk and drive, on several occasions I loaded them and their boards in the van and drove them to the Gulf, but I couldn't do anything with them. I could only watch. They seemed to understand, but it was still hard on me.

I have no doubt that there are things my sons probably wanted to do, but they never mentioned them for fear of putting me in a situation where I'd have to decide whether I might hurt myself. So I do feel that my boys were cheated out of normal boy things in their growing up years.

Nicole, being a girl, had that "Daddy thing." She was our oldest child. She expressed her feelings very differently from Joe, who is a very emotional kid. Chris is the cool one, although deeply sensitive, and doesn't show his feelings as easily as his twin.

While writing this book, I asked my kids to tell me how the accident affected them and our family and how it changed their perception of me. When the accident happened in 1989, Nicole was thirteen years old. Here is her response:

> The biggest impact on my life was living away from my parents for several months. I lived with the Mauldin family from our church during that time. The accident taught me to appreciate my own family. I'm very close to all of them, because I realize how fortunate I was to be a part of such a wonderful family. I also feel that I am able to help people in crisis situations because I learned at a young age how to use prayer and friends to help me get through difficult times. It caused me to look at life in a different way. At a young age I was able to realize that life is precious, and that we have to seize every moment.
>
> I feel that our family is very close because of the accident. I also feel we really look after one another, and that we would do anything for our family members. The boys and I have a special bond that we don't always see between brothers and sisters. Daddy's accident and recovery taught us to be there for each other. Mom became a lot stronger and independent, because Dad couldn't take care of the things he always had. I

only wish Daddy didn't have to go through this to bring us so close together.

After Dad was hurt so bad, I saw for the first time that he was a vulnerable person. Before the accident, he had seemed indestructible. Over the years since, I have seen that the accident has made him even stronger. He may have been hurt physically, but he is the strongest person I know spiritually and emotionally. To have gone through what he did and still be such a loving and devoted servant of God is amazing to me.

For a long time I was angry about the accident, but I grew up and realized how fortunate we are to still have him and how the accident brought us closer. If he had died in that accident I don't know how I would have made it through some of the toughest times in my life. There is something very special about getting advice from someone who has been to heaven, survived countless surgeries, and lived to tell about it. I tend to listen a little harder to him now.

Joe was eight years old at the time of the accident, and this is how he responded:

My first memory was being picked up by a teacher friend of my mother's. When I saw my mom crying, I knew something was very wrong.

I remember going to the hospital to see Dad. They showed us a doll made up to look like Dad's injuries, so when we went in we would be prepared. It was really hard to see Dad like that. We didn't stay long, which was fine with me because I did not like seeing him that way. Chris and I had to move in with our grandparents in Louisiana. I thought it was cool at first, but then I started to miss my family. I'm really glad I had my twin brother with me. Every weekend we drove from Bossier City to Houston. That got old very fast.

The worst thing about the accident was that while other kids were going camping and fishing with their dads, I never got to experience those things. I still think about that a lot even today.

Sometimes I feel kind of angry and cheated or depressed. But in the past few years, I've gotten to go camping and fishing with Dad. I'm not sure that he realizes how happy that makes me. Through this experience I realized how many people loved and cared about our family. If we hadn't had God in our lives, I don't know how we would have gotten through this.

This is Chris's response:

When you're an eight-year-old, your father is a superhero. He's invincible. When I first heard about Dad's accident, I didn't think it was nearly as serious as it turned out to be. Mom was upset when she told me the news and couldn't hide the tears. But Dad was strong, and I'd never seen him cry. Even when I saw him surrounded by monitors in the ICU, hooked up to oxygen, and barely able to speak, I fully expected him to be home in a week.

I wasn't present for most of the major surgeries. I went to live with my grandparents only days after the accident and saw my dad only on weekends. During those brief encounters, I began to understand just how bad he hurt—both his body and his spirit.

I was fascinated by the metal contraptions that surrounded his left arm and leg, but I knew they caused him immense pain. He looked so worn out as if he had just woken up, or maybe could never quite fall asleep. Sometimes I got the impression he didn't want me or anyone else in the room. Even as little as I understood about depression, I knew he was suffering from it.

The first thing I did each time I visited him was to approach slowly and put my arms around him. I hugged him gently. For the first time in my life, he seemed fragile. Even when he returned home from the hospital, I continued the same routine—come home from school and hug Dad. It was as much to reassure me as it was to comfort him. I hope it served both purposes.

As my brother, Joe, and I grew older, and Dad's recovery continued, we became more interested in sports and the outdoors. Dad would do his best to join us. I remember feeling terrible when I threw the football too far for Dad's reach. He'd stumble and sometimes he'd fall. I choked back tears on a number of occasions. I'm sure he did the same. But from an emotional standpoint, Dad was always there for me. He is vitally interested in what his kids do. After all, I suppose we make his return from Paradise worthwhile in some regard.

The family grew closer as a result of Dad's accident. We all took different roles out of sheer necessity. Mom became the decision maker and disciplinarian during Dad's recovery. I tried my best to be the man of the house. Sometimes I was really just a bully, but I grew out of it. I learned to lean on the others as they leaned on me. Nicole mothered Joe and me as best she could.

Dad suffered from depression for years after the accident—still does to some extent. Maybe he struggled with it before the accident, but if he did, I never noticed. Dad is fiercely independent and seldom lets his family into his darkest corners. I guess I'm the same way.

Here is Eva's response to how her perception of me has changed:

I was most surprised by Don's lack of determination during the initial days following the wreck. He had always been a fighter, one who was constantly pushing himself and others to do more. When he wouldn't try to breathe it was almost as if I didn't know him. The depression had also been a new aspect. I learned to recognize the sign of a "bad time" approaching. It is harder when the pain is worse; he doesn't sleep and the stress builds.

Through the years I've learned that if I leave Don alone he eventually returns to a more even keel. When I wanted to tell him something he really needed to hear but didn't want to know, I had to bite my tongue—and on a few occasions I didn't succeed.

Today, I don't think of him as injured, even though I know he is and always will be. Don goes at such a pace that it is easy for me to forget his pain and handicaps. My husband is truly a remarkable person.

My kids were probably more confident about my recovery than I was. They never saw me receiving therapy, agonizing, or throwing up because I'd gotten so sick, or seen me when I tried to stand up too fast. As much as possible, we tried to insulate them. Eva saw me at my worst, but she protected the children as much as possible.

Although they don't admit it, there probably is a "Dad gap" for my children, especially the twins. Because they were eight years old, they missed my being there for an important developmental time to help them learn to do things such as play team sports and go camping.

Looking back, I think the accident affected my parents more permanently than anybody. In fact, they were devastated. I'm the oldest of three sons, and all of us had been healthy. Then, suddenly, when I reached the age of thirty-eight, they were heartbroken and felt helpless to do anything for me. For a long time, they thought I would probably die.

My dad had been a career military man, and my mother had to learn to handle just about everything. Yet when they came to see me during the first week in the hospital, Mom fainted. Dad grabbed her and helped her out of the room. She wasn't prepared to see me in such bad shape. I'm not sure anyone would have been.

Even now, I'm not sure my mother has fully recovered from my accident. But here are two of many very beautiful memories of my parents' devotion to me.

First, during the summer following the accident, as if Eva didn't have enough to concern herself with, she decided to take the South Park youth to summer camp. That would have been my job had I been physically able. But she tackled it with gusto. That meant someone would have to stay with me while she was away.

My mother cheerfully agreed to do so. The week of the church youth camp came, and Eva left me with Mom. Each day Mother prepared meals for me, and I was so glad to have her there. But I did dread one daily occurrence—my mother would be required to empty my urinals and bedpans. Now, I know she had diapered me when I was a baby, but a lot of time had passed between infant powderings and the present.

I remember the first time I had to go when she was caring for me, and I asked for the bedpan. She acted as if it were the most natural thing ever. After I had finished, I agonized over having to tell her.

She saved me the embarrassment by asking if I was through. I just nodded. She took the bedpan into the bathroom, and then I heard one of the most remarkable sounds I have ever heard in my life. After she entered the bathroom and flushed the commode, I could hear my mother singing. In spite of the most lowly of tasks one human can perform for another, she sang as she washed out the bedpan. It was as if her whole motherhood was wrapped up in that moment. She was again doing something for her son that he could not do for himself, and she was happy and fulfilled. I will cherish that memory, for it defines the devotion that only a mother could have.

Second, I remember one private moment I had with my father, equally poignant and dramatic. One day, following yet another 250-mile trip to see me for an afternoon at St. Luke's, my parents were preparing for the return trip to their home near Bossier City.

For some reason I don't recall, Mom had stepped out of the room. Alone now, my father came close to my bed and took my only unbroken limb, my right hand, in his gnarled hand. He leaned close to me and with great emotion and absolute honesty said, "I would give anything to trade places with you and take this on me."

He's my dad, and more than at any other time, I realized how much he loves me.

⟋⟍

Repeatedly, my doctor has told me, "Everything we did for you is the best we can do. Don't count on being able to live a long, productive life. Because of arthritis and a lot of other complications that will set in, you're going to have an uphill battle to be even as mobile as you are now."

He knew what he was talking about. It's been fifteen years since my accident. I've already felt the beginning of arthritis. Weather changes affect me; I grow tired faster. Some of it may be age, but I think it's a reflection of the fact that I have to use my legs and knees in ways God didn't design them to be used.

Even today, my left knee hyperextends, so if someone comes from behind and inadvertently slaps me on the back, I have to catch myself or I'll keep going forward. I can't lock my knee into place to keep from losing my balance and pitching forward.

I've tried to make light of this, quipping, "I've fallen in some of the best places in Texas." Or, "I've considered commissioning some little plaques that say, 'Don Piper fell here.'"

One time I led an outdoor conference in the Texas hill country. The ground was uneven and I'd walk along and all of a sudden, I'd fall. I wasn't hurt, but I fell three times the first day.

Despite everything they did for me, one of my legs is an inch and a half shorter than the other. That alone makes my backbone curve. The backbone is beginning to show wear and tear, as are my hip joints. My left elbow is so messed up I can't straighten it out. Doctors did everything they could, including operating on it several times. The elbow was fractured on the inside, and when it knitted back together, it wouldn't allow me to straighten it. To use the doctor's expression, "It's a very gimpy joint."

An injury like that, he pointed out, is not forgiving. Once it gets messed up, it's hard to fix it again.

This is part of my new normal.

Once after a visit to Dr. Tom Greider's office, he asked me back into his private suite. Despite his busy caseload, I felt he was genuinely interested in me, and we talked about a lot of things.

On a whim I asked, "Tom, just how bad was I when they brought me in that night of the accident?"

He didn't flinch. "I've seen worse." He paused for a moment, leaned over his desk, and then continued, "But none of them lived."

I've had to find different ways to do things. I am alive, however, and I intend to serve Jesus Christ as long as I remain alive. But I already know what's ahead, waiting for me.

I'm ready to leave this earth anytime.

15

TOUCHING LIVES

All praise to the God and Father of our Lord Jesus Christ. He is the source of every mercy and the God who comforts us. He comforts us in all our troubles so that we can comfort others. When others are troubled, we will be able to give them the same comfort God has given us.

2 Corinthians 1:3–4

Sometimes I still ask God why I wasn't allowed to stay in heaven. I have no answer to that question. I have learned, however, that God brings people into my life who need me or need to hear my message, giving me the opportunity to touch their lives.

One of the first times I was able to minister to someone as a result of my accident was when I was the guest preacher in a large church. They invited me specifically to talk about my trip to heaven. A woman who sat near the front and to my left began to weep shortly after I began to speak. I could see the tears sliding down her cheeks. As soon as we closed the meeting, she rushed up to me and clasped my hand.

"My mother died last week."

"I'm so sorry for your loss—"

"No, no, you don't understand. God sent you here tonight. I needed this kind of reassurance. Not that I didn't believe—I did, but my heart has been so heavy because of the loss. I feel so much better. She *is* in a better place. Oh, Reverend Piper, I needed to hear that tonight."

Before I could say anything more, she hugged me and added, "God also sent *me* here tonight because I needed this reassurance. Not that I didn't believe and didn't know—because I'm a believer and so was she—but I needed to hear those words tonight. I needed to know about heaven from someone who had been there."

So far as I recall, she was the first to talk to me that way, but certainly not the last. I've heard this kind of response hundreds of times. It still amazes me that I can be a blessing to so many just by sharing my experience.

For those who already believe, my testimony has been reassuring; for skeptics, it's opened them up to think more seriously about God.

~

Two years after the accident, when I still wore leg braces and walked with crutches, I took a group of our young people to a conference at Houston's First Baptist Church. Dawson McAllister, a great teacher to youth, was the speaker. He's so popular he fills up the place.

As happens when you work with teens, we were late in leaving South Park Church. I didn't say anything, but I felt extremely irritated with the delay. I had wanted to arrive early because I knew the best seats would be taken if we didn't get there at least an hour before starting time.

I tried not to let it show, but I was still upset by the time we reached First Baptist Church in Houston. Once we went inside the huge building, we realized—as I had expected—that all the seats on the lower floor were filled. We'd have to climb the stairs.

I groaned at the thought of having to do more walking. Even though I was mobile, wearing those braces and the pressure of the crutches under my armpits tired me out. To make it worse, the elevator wasn't working. *If that person hadn't been late*, I kept thinking, *I wouldn't have to hobble up all those stairs.*

It wasn't just clumping up the stairs, but the auditorium was so full that the only places left to sit were in the top rows. Our young people, naturally, raced ahead to claim those seats. They promised to save one for me on the end. I counted 150 steps as I painfully made my way up.

By the time I finally reached the top, exhaustion had overcome me. I could hardly walk the last flight and across the back of the auditorium to the seat the kids had saved for me. Before I sat down—which also demanded a lot of effort—I rested by leaning against the wall. As I tried to catch my breath, I asked myself, *What am I doing here?*

I could have gotten other adults to take the kids, but I really wanted to be with them. I wanted to feel useful again. I also knew this would be an exciting event for the youth, and I wanted to be part of it. Boisterous laughter and shouting back and forth filled the place. The youth were ready to be blessed and challenged, but at that moment, I didn't think about the kids or how much they would get out of the meeting. I thought only of being worn out.

At that moment self-pity took over. As I continued to lean against the wall, my gaze swept the auditorium. Two sections over I spotted a teenage boy in a wheelchair. He was sitting with his head in his hands, his back to me. As I stared at him, I *knew* I had to go over and talk to him. Suddenly I didn't question my actions and I forgot about being tired.

I leaned my crutches against the wall and then slowly, painfully made my way across to his section and down the steps.

He was a large, good-looking kid, maybe sixteen years old. When I got closer, I realized why I needed to talk to him. He was wearing an Ilizarov frame—which I hadn't been able to see from where I had stood. My tiredness vanished, along with my anger and self-pity. It was as if I saw myself in that wheelchair and reexperienced all the pain of those days.

He was looking away from me when I laid my hand on his shoulder. His head spun around and he glared at me.

"That really hurts doesn't it?" I asked.

He looked at me as if to say, *What kind of fool are you?* Instead he said, "Yeah. It hurts very much."

"I know." I patted his shoulder. "Believe me, I know."

His eyes widened. "You do?"

"I do. I had one too."

"It's horrible."

"I know that. It's just horrible. I wore one on my left leg for eleven months."

"Nobody ever understands," he said plaintively.

"They can't. It's not something you can talk about and have anyone understand your pain."

For the first time I saw something in his eyes. Maybe it was hope, or maybe just a sense of peace because at long last he had found someone who knew what he was going through. We had connected, and I felt privileged to be standing next to him.

"My name is Don," I said, "and you've just met somebody who understands the pain and the discouragement you're going through."

He stared at me, and then his eyes moistened. "I don't know if I'm going to make it."

"You're going to make it. Trust me, you'll make it."

"Maybe," he said.

"What happened?" By then I'd realized it hadn't been a voluntary surgery.

"I had a ski accident."

I noticed that he was wearing a letter jacket. I asked, "You a football player?"

"Yes, sir."

Briefly I told him about my accident, and he told me more about what had happened to him. "I'm going to tell you something," I said. "One day you will walk again."

His face registered skepticism.

"You might not play football again, but you'll walk." I handed him my business card. "My number is on the card, and you can call me anytime, day or night, twenty-four hours a day."

He took the card and stared at it.

"I'm going to walk back up there to my kids." I pointed to where they sat. "I want you to watch me. And as you watch, I want you to know that one day you will walk too." I laughed. "And I'll bet you'll walk better than I do."

He reached up, grabbed me, and hugged me. He held me tight for a long time. I could feel his constricted breathing as he fought back tears. Finally he released me and mumbled his thanks.

"You've found somebody who understands," I said. "Please call me."

That boy needed somebody who understood. I don't know that I had much to offer, but I had my experience and I could talk to him about pain. Had I not gone through it myself, I'd just be telling him, "I hope you feel better. You're going to be okay"—well-meaning words that most people used.

When I reached the top row, perspiration drenched my body from all the effort, but I didn't care. I turned around. He still stared at me. I smiled and waved, and he waved back. The dejection and despair had left his face.

Over the next six months, I received three calls from him, two just to talk and one late at night when he was really discouraged.

They were phone calls I will always cherish, one struggling pilgrim to another.

⟶

One time, a Houston TV station scheduled me to appear on a live talk show. While I was waiting in their greenroom, the producer came in and began to explain how the show worked and some of the questions I could expect to be asked.

"That's fine," I said. "Who else is a guest on the show?"

"You're it."

"Wait a minute. You're going to do an hour-long show and I'm the only guest?"

"That's right."

I wondered what I would talk about for an hour. It was fairly early in my recovery, and at the time I had no idea how interested people were in my story. By then the doctor had removed the Ilizarov frame and I was wearing braces and using crutches. I had brought pictures of me in the hospital, which they televised that day. And I brought the Ilizarov device itself.

Once the TV interview started, I told my story, and then the host asked me questions. The hour passed quickly. While we were still live on the show, a woman called the TV station and insisted, "I need to talk to Reverend Piper immediately."

They wouldn't interrupt the program, but as soon as the program ended, someone handed me a slip of paper with her telephone number. I called her.

"You've got to talk to my brother," she said.

"What's the matter with him?"

"He was involved in a fight in a bar, and another man pulled out a shotgun and blew his leg off. He's wearing one of those things like you used to have on your leg."

"Of course I'll talk to him," I said. "Where is he?"

"He's home in bed."

"Give me the address and I'll go—"

"Oh no, you can't go over there. He's angry and mean. And he's violent. He won't talk to anybody who comes to see him." She gave me his telephone number. "Please call him, but he's so mean right now, I guarantee that he'll cuss you out." Then she added, "And he may just hang up on you, but try him anyway. Please."

As soon as I got home, I called her brother and introduced myself. Before I had spoken more than three sentences, he did just what she had predicted. He yelled at me. He screamed and let me have it with just about every swear word I'd ever heard, and he repeated them several times.

When he paused I said quietly, "I had one of those things on my leg that you have—that fixator."

He didn't say anything for a few seconds, so I said, "I wore one of those Ilizarov devices on my left leg. I know what you must be going through."

"Oh, man, this is killing me. It hurts all the time. It's just—" and he went off again as if he hadn't heard me, peppering his anger with a lot of profanity.

When he paused again, I said, "I understand what it feels like to have one of them."

"You don't have it anymore?"

"No, I finally got it off. If you do what you're supposed to do, you can get yours off one day." That didn't sound like much, but it was the only thing I could think to say.

"If I had some wrenches I'd take it off right now."

"If you take it off, you might as well cut your leg off, because it's the only thing that's holding your leg on."

"I know that, but it's just killing me. I can't sleep—" Then he went on again, telling me how miserable he was and how much he hated everything.

Then something occurred to me, and I interrupted him. "What does your leg look like? Does it seem to be hot near the pinholes? Is it the same color up and down your skin? Are there certain holes that hurt more than others?"

"Yeah, that's right. One of them especially—man, it hurts real bad."

"Is your sister there yet?" When he said she was, I ordered him, "Put her on the phone."

He didn't argue and she picked up the phone. "Thank you," she said. "I appreciate so—"

"Listen to me," I said, interrupting her. "I want you to call an ambulance *right now*. Take your brother to the hospital as fast as you can get there. He has a serious infection in that leg. If he doesn't get there soon, he's going to lose his leg."

"You think so?"

"I'm telling you. He has all the symptoms. He's probably got a fever too. Have you checked?"

"Yes, that's right. He's running a fever."

"Get him to the hospital immediately. Call me afterward."

The next day she called. "Oh, you were right! He has an infection, and he was in terrible shape. They gave him all those antibiotics. They said he got there just in time, and he's doing better today."

"I assume he's still in the isolation unit." When she said he was, I added, "I'm going to come and see him."

As a minister I could get in to see him. I went to the hospital, talked to him, and prayed with him. Eventually that young man turned to Jesus Christ.

If I hadn't been on that TV show and his sister hadn't watched it, he might not have only lost a leg; there is a strong possibility that he would have died. Not only had God used me to save the young man's physical life but I had been an instrument in his salvation. That was just one more instance of my beginning to see that God still has things for me to do here on earth.

I had immediately recognized the problem because it had happened to me when I was still in the hospital. I had gotten an infection and began hurting badly. I thought it was just part of the pain I'd have to go through. Then a nurse discovered that I had an infection in one of those pinholes.

I remembered then how days before, one of the nurses apparently had cross-contaminated the pinholes. She was a surly type and never showed me compassion like the others. She came in and did her work, but she acted as if she resented having to work with me.

They used Q-tips, and they had been instructed to use a new one to clean each hole. I had noticed that this time, the nurse didn't get a fresh Q-tip each time, probably because it was faster not to reach for a new one. I didn't think anything about that until after the hole became infected. My added pain had come about because of her laziness. Once they discovered the infection and my elevated temperature, they rushed me into the isolation unit, where I stayed for two weeks. While I was there, no one could visit me.

Eva complained and told the doctor what happened. I never saw that nurse again, so I don't know if they fired her or transferred her.

—

As much as I enjoy public speaking, few opportunities excite me more than speaking at my alma mater, Louisiana State University (LSU). My wife and I met at LSU, and two of our three children also studied there.

One of the on-campus organizations where I have spoken on several occasions is the Baptist Collegiate Ministry (BCM). While Nicole was a student at LSU and served as one of the officers in that group, the BCM invited me to speak. Knowing she would be in the audience made the experience even more delightful.

Among the many campus activities the BCM sponsored was a Thursday night praise and worship service called TNT. The committee asked me to speak to them about my accident.

The students advertised my talk all over campus as "Dead Man Talking." Because so many showed up, they scheduled two back-to-back services. As I spoke, the audience seemed mesmerized by the story of a man who died and came back to life. I spoke of heaven, answered prayer, and miracles. I told them about singing "What a Friend We Have in Jesus" in the car with Dick Onerecker.

As each service ended, the praise band led us in a chorus of that meaningful song. I didn't know they were going to do it. While I have no doubt they were led by the Spirit to do so, "What a Friend We Have in Jesus" remains a difficult song for me to hear or sing.

Afterward a large number of students waited around to ask questions. Among them was an African-American student named Walter Foster. He asked many questions himself and stayed and listened to the other students' questions as well. When I left the auditorium, Walter followed me. Although I didn't mind, I felt as if he pursued me with dogged determination—as if he couldn't get enough details about heaven or hear enough about my experience.

A few months later, Nicole called me. "Do you remember Walter Foster?" Her voice broke and she started to cry. As soon as I said I remembered him, she said, "He . . . he died. He suffered a heart attack! Just like that—and he was gone."

Apparently Walter had known about his serious heart condition and was under medical care; everyone assumed he was doing all right. Obviously his death shocked all the students who knew him.

"Twenty-year-old students aren't supposed to die," one of his friends had said.

After I hung up the phone, I thought back to the day when Walter and I met. I wondered if he had had a premonition about his death. The fact that he followed me the whole time I was at LSU and plied me with endless questions about heaven caused me to wonder. His questions seemed more than just curiosity. *Maybe,* I thought, *even then God was preparing him for his homeward journey.*

His sudden death devastated his friends, especially those involved with the Baptist Collegiate Ministry. They were a close-knit group and mourned the loss of their dear member. The night following his death, they gathered at the BCM building—the place Walter loved most.

During an emotional meeting that night, a number of his friends spoke at length about how much it had meant to Walter that I had shared my experience about heaven. Many mentioned the excitement he expressed to them over what he had heard. He talked about it for days afterward.

"Several times during the day when Reverend Piper was here," one of them said, "Walter told me, 'One day I know I'm going to be in heaven myself!'"

Pressing church business kept me from being at Walter's memorial service at First Baptist Church of Baton Rouge. Nicole represented our family and reported that evening about the celebration of Walter's life. Two special requests from his friends were that the preacher would share the gospel message and that someone would sing one particular song. Of course, it was "What a Friend We Have in Jesus." The audience learned the special significance that hymn held for Walter.

Nicole, a music major at LSU and an excellent soloist, sang the song to the assembled mourners. They responded with both great sadness and glorious hope. Tears flowed and many smiled peacefully.

After the service, many students lingered to talk about how much Walter's unwavering belief in heaven had comforted and encouraged them.

One of the other bright things to emerge from my testimony at the BCM and Walter's later passing was the construction and dedication of a prayer garden at the LSU BCM. That seems appropriate to me, because each time I share my story, I stress the paramount importance of prayer. After all, I'm still alive because of answered prayer.

Like many others whose lives have divinely intersected with mine since my accident and my return from heaven, Walter represents those who will be waiting for me the next time God calls me home.

—

Sue Fayle's first husband died of cancer. His long torturous passing took a lot out of her. She assumed she would live the rest of her life as a widow. But her neighbor Charles, also without a spouse, changed that. They were not only neighbors, but in their common sense of loss, they became good friends. As time passed, they seemed to fulfill needs for each other in a way that only those who have loved and lost seem to understand. Their friendship evolved into love, and they cautiously considered marriage.

Sue had serious reservations about marrying Charles because he came from what she called a rough-and-tough working-class neighborhood. He had a history of hard drinking, and she said, "I can't live with that."

As their love continued to grow, however, Sue issued one simple condition for marriage: "I won't marry a man who gets drunk."

Charles not only stopped getting drunk, he quit drinking altogether. Now they were ready to talk of marriage.

One day they talked about the death of their spouses—both of whom had died of cancer. "If I'm ever diagnosed with cancer," he said, "I'll kill myself." He knew that not only did the person with the disease suffer but their loved ones went through deep agony as well. "I couldn't put anyone through that ordeal."

They did marry, had a good marriage, and Charles never drank again. Sue had already been active in our church, but after their marriage, Charles also became active.

One day, however, he received the one diagnosis he feared most of all: He had cancer. Now he had to face his deep-seated terror. He was afraid that his diagnosis would put Sue through the same terrible ordeal she had faced before.

He also faced another fear after he received the diagnosis: The news forced him to confront his own mortality. "I'm terrified of dying," he confessed. Although Charles was a church member and said he believed, he was one of those individuals who doubted his salvation. Sue assured him that while she was dedicated to seeing him through this crisis, she was concerned about his lack of assurance of his salvation. She had heard my testimony about heaven on several occasions and had retold my story to others.

"Can you talk to Charles?" she asked me one day. "He needs to hear your testimony from you."

By then I had become the single adult minister of Pasadena's First Baptist Church, where I am today. Sue and I had worked together on projects on many occasions.

"Please talk to him about salvation, but also tell him about what life is like after death. I believe that a man-to-man talk with Charles would do a lot for him."

I knew Charles, of course, and because of his past, I suspected he thought he wasn't good enough for God. I agreed to talk to him.

Charles and I hit it off right away. He was a great guy and easy to relate to. I made it a point to visit him on a regular basis. Whenever I came, Sue excused herself and stayed out of the room until I was ready to leave.

Even as Charles's health deteriorated, he never displayed the least bit of anger or depression. We even talked about how difficult it was to be dependent on others for even the most personal of functions—bedpans, urinals, and bathing.

About the fourth time I visited, Charles finally opened up. "I'm afraid. I want to go to heaven, but I need assurance—I want to be certain that when I die, I'll go to heaven."

As he talked about his life, it was obvious that his experience with God was authentic. As is often the case, for many years before he married Sue, he simply hadn't been a faithful follower of Christ. Several times I reminded him of the verses in the Bible that promise heaven as the ultimate destination for all believers.

"I know, I know," he said. "Before I was saved, I knew I wouldn't go to heaven. I was going to hell. Now I want to be sure about heaven."

My description of heaven encouraged him. "Yes, yes, that's what I want," he said.

On one visit as he talked, he smiled and said, "I'm ready. I'm at peace. I finally know that I'll go to heaven."

On both of the last two visits I made, Charles said, "Tell me again. Tell me once more what heaven is like."

I told him again, even though he had already heard everything I had to say. It was as if his assurance grew each time I talked about heaven.

A short time before he died, Sue put Charles in hospice at the Houston Medical Center, just a few doors away from where I had been hospitalized for such a long time.

On the last day of his life on earth, Charles told Sue, "It's going to be all right. I'm going from pain to peace. Someday we'll be together again."

When Sue called and told me, she added, "He died absolutely without fear."

Charles's calm assurance and acceptance gave Sue peace as she worked through her own grief and loss. She told me that only weeks before his death, he'd said listening to my experience and seeing the positive glow in my life made the difference. "It's settled," he'd said. "I know I'm going to a better place."

As Sue shared her memories of Charles, she laughed and said, "Won't I be the lucky one? I've got two men waiting for me. One day, when my time comes, I'll have one on each arm, former husbands who are also brothers in Christ, and they can escort me down the streets of gold."

———

When Joe, one of my twins, reached his teens, we decided to look for a used car for him. He wanted a truck, so we searched until we found one he liked, a 1993 Ford Ranger.

The dealer's name was Gary Emmons; he owned a longtime automobile dealership in our area. Once we settled on the truck Joe wanted, we went inside to make the deal. Mr. Emmons gave us an excellent price, and Joe bought the truck.

Because of that experience, a good relationship formed between Gary Emmons and my family. We bought three or four more cars from him after that.

Gary knew a little about what had happened to me, but no details. He was a race-car driver as well as a car dealer. He seemed fascinated with my story. He had said he'd like to hear the whole story one day, but either he was too busy or I had to rush on.

One day Joe went to the dealership to make a payment. Gary waved him over. "You'll never believe this." The man grinned. "An amazing thing happened yesterday."

"What?"

"I went to check out a car that we had just bought. I got inside the car to do the things I usually do—you know, punch all the buttons to see if everything works—things like listen to the engine for any defects, check the air conditioner, and see if the radio works. I noticed a tape inside the cassette deck. I pushed the eject button."

He paused and smiled. "Bet you'll never guess what was on that tape."

"I have no idea," Joe said.

"It was your dad's story. We had bought the car in an auction, so there was no owner to give the tape back to. I took the tape and listened to it. The only thing I could think of when I heard it was one word—*awesome*."

As I look back, it's amazing. Gary had wanted to hear my story, but we just had not gotten together.

"What are the odds of my going to an automobile auction with thousands of cars for sale," Gary asked Joe, "then I sit inside one, push a button, and hear your dad talking?"

For days after that, I think Gary must have told everybody he talked to about my accident.

Of course, that testimony thrilled me. I've also heard many other stories of the way God has used my story.

I had made a tape about my experience while preaching in my church, Pasadena's First Baptist, and had it duplicated. I must have distributed thousands of them. I also know people took the tape and copied it for their friends. I know people who ordered as many as twenty tapes over a period of months.

That testimonial tape just keeps going on and on. Many people who heard my story duplicated it for people going through physical trauma themselves or those who are dealing with the loss of a loved one.

I can only conclude that God had a plan for Gary Emmons to hear that tape and made sure he did.

⌒

One day while I was walking down the hallway of First Baptist Church of Pasadena, a woman stopped me. That's not unusual, of course. In fact, my wife jokes that it takes me thirty minutes to walk twenty feet because everyone has something he or she needs to ask me or tell me. We have over ten thousand members; that's a lot of folks to get around to.

"Oh, Reverend Piper, I came by just to see you. I want to tell you something—something that I think you need to hear."

Usually when someone starts out that way, he usually adds, "It's for your own good," and it's usually not something I want to hear. Several other people were with me, and I wasn't sure how to react. As I stared at her, however, I sensed an urgency in her face and a deep intensity. I turned to the others and asked, "Would you mind?"

They were gracious, of course.

"I'm a registered nurse, and you will never believe what happened."

"I've had a lot of unbelievable things happen. Just try me."

"This happened at the hospital. A woman's mother, who was very ill and hospitalized, was able to hear your tape, and it changed her life."

I had heard that before, but I never minded hearing new stories, so I said, "Tell me more."

"Somebody brought her this tape and she wasn't a believer. But the person wanted her to listen to the tape anyway. Her friends had tried to talk to her about God. They had given her Bibles, all kinds of books and pamphlets, but nothing affected her. She said, 'I don't want to talk about God, religion, or salvation.' Even though she was terminally ill, she wasn't open to any message about eternity."

She paused to wipe a tear from her eyes before she continued, "Somebody brought her a tape—your tape about your

176

experience in heaven—and asked her if she would listen to it. The friend didn't press it, but said something casual like, 'You might find this helpful. It's about a man who died, went to heaven, and came back to life again.'"

The nurse told me that the woman said that she might listen to it if she thought about it. The friend left. The tape lay on the stand next to her bed, unheard. Her health soon deteriorated so badly that doctors told her daughter that it was only a matter of a week, two at the most.

The daughter, who was a believer, desperately wanted her mother to hear the tape of my testimony. The tape contains two messages. The first side tells of the miracles that had to happen for me to live, and recounts the answered prayer that took place for me to live—as I've written about earlier in this book. The second side of the tape tells about what heaven is like. I called it "The Cure for Heart Trouble." That's the part the daughter wanted her mother to listen to.

But the woman refused. "I don't want to listen to all that stuff," she said.

Days went by, and the older woman's condition grew more desperate. The nurse who was talking to me, and who was a Christian, realized what was going on. After she talked with the daughter, the nurse decided to talk to the patient herself about her soul—something she had not done before. She reasoned that sometimes it's easier for a stranger or someone less known to give a positive witness than it is for a family member.

After working her shift, the nurse walked into the room and asked, "May I sit down and talk to you a few minutes?"

The dying woman nodded.

Gently and discreetly the nurse talked about faith and God's peace and how much of a difference Jesus Christ had made in her own life.

The whole time, the woman said nothing.

The nurse mentioned the tape. "I've heard it, and I think it's something you would like to know. Would you like to listen to the tape?"

The old woman nodded, so the nurse put the tape in the cassette recorder and left.

The next day the dying woman told her daughter and the nurse that she had listened to the tape. "I found it very interesting. I'm seriously thinking about becoming a Christian."

Even though the nurse and the daughter rejoiced, they didn't try to pressure the dying woman. Two days passed before the woman said, "I have become a believer." She told her daughter first and then the nurse. After that, no matter who came into the room to see her, the dying woman would say, "I have become a Christian. I've accepted Jesus Christ as my Savior and I'm going to heaven."

Within hours after her publicly telling others about her conversion, the woman's condition deteriorated. She drifted in and out of consciousness. The next day when the nurse came on duty, she learned that the old woman had died only minutes earlier.

The nurse told me all of that and then said, "You won't believe what was happening during those final moments while she was dying."

Before I could ask, she said, "The tape recorder was on the bed beside her, and her daughter had put in the second side of your tape where you describe heaven. As her life drifted away, she was listening to your account of what heaven is like. The last thing she heard before she left this world to join God in heaven was a description of heaven."

Despite my trying to remain stoic, tears seeped from the corners of my eyes.

"I just thought you'd like to know that."

"Yes," I said. "Thank you for telling me. That's great encouragement for me."

As she retold some of the story to those with me, I thanked God for bringing me back to earth. "Oh, God, I do see some purpose in my staying here. Thank you for allowing me to hear this story."

One time I preached at the Chocolate Bayou Baptist Church, south of Houston. They had asked me to share my death-and-heaven experience.

I was getting my final thoughts together. Typically, in Baptist churches, they have a soloist or some kind of special music just before the guest speaker comes to the pulpit. A woman, who had not been in the service and apparently didn't know what I was going to talk about, came in from a side door to sing.

She had a lovely voice and began to sing a song called "Broken and Spilled Out" about the alabaster jar the woman used when she washed Jesus' feet.

As soon as she sat down, I stood up and began to tell them about my accident. I didn't make any connection between her song and my message, but I noticed that several people kept frowning at the woman.

After the service, I heard someone say to the soloist, "That was an interesting song about being broken and spilled out for you to sing before Don talked." The way he said the word *interesting* really meant *tasteless*.

"Oh!" she said. The shock on her face made me aware that she hadn't known what I was going to speak about. Obviously, she hadn't made the connection either.

Our eyes met and she started to cry. "I'm sorry . . . I'm sorry."

"That's fine," I said. "Really, it's all right." I started to walk on.

"Broken and spilled," someone said. "That's what happened to you, wasn't it?" At least a dozen people made similar comments. A few assumed we had planned for her to sing that particular song.

I stopped and looked back. The soloist stood next to the piano, and she was crying. I excused myself and walked back to her. "That's a beautiful song about a wonderful experience. You didn't know what I was going to talk about, but that's all right, because I can't think of a better song."

She smiled in gratefulness and started to apologize again. "It's fine. Really, it's fine," I assured her.

As I walked away, I thought maybe I had been broken and spilled out. But I smiled at another idea: *I'm also being put back together again.*

16

FINDING PURPOSE

I am convinced of this, so I will continue with you so that you will grow and experience the joy of your faith.

Philippians 1:25

B rad Turpin, a motorcycle police officer from the Houston suburb of Pasadena, almost lost a leg. His police motorcycle crashed into the back of a flatbed truck. He would have bled out on the concrete if the EMTs hadn't applied a tourniquet to his leg.

Sonny Steed, the former minister of education at our church, knew Brad personally and asked me to go see him. "Absolutely," I said, especially after I heard that he would be wearing a fixator. I called and made sure he'd let me come. I don't know why, but just before we left, I picked up pictures showing my accident and my recovery.

Sonny drove me to the officer's house. Once we had walked inside, it was almost like seeing the way my living room had looked for months. Brad was lying in a hospital bed with the trapeze bar above him. His device was similar, but not quite the same as mine, because in the dozen years since my accident, technology had improved.

Other people were there, so I sat down and joined in casual conversation. He was nice enough, but I knew he'd seen so many people he was tired of visitors. As soon as the last visitor left, I said, "You really are tired of talking to people aren't you?"

Brad nodded.

"I understand. You almost feel like you're on display here. The phone never stops ringing. Everybody wants to come by to see you."

He nodded again. "I appreciate them coming, but I need some peace and quiet."

"I apologize for interrupting you, but Sonny brought me by to see you because I wanted to talk to you about what to expect. I pointed to the Ilizarov and said, "I had one of these external fixators."

"Oh, you did?"

I showed him my pictures, beginning with those taken the day after they put on the Ilizarov frame. Each one showed progression to the next step. He stared at each one closely and saw that I had been worse off than he was.

"And you recovered, didn't you?"

"Yes, I did, and so will you."

"That's good that you made it all right, but I don't think I'm going to make it. They can't give me any guarantee that I'm going to keep this leg. The doctors are pessimistic, so that makes it harder for me."

"Well, that's just the way they are," I said, remembering so well my feelings in those early days. "They try to err on the side of being conservative and try not to get your hopes up. Months from now, they know, you could have this fixator and everything could be working fine and then your leg could get infected and you could still lose it."

"That's what I mean. I'm just not sure it's worth all this pain."

"The good news is that the pain will ease up as you get better."

His wife had walked in during the conversation and listened. "I'm just so tired at the lack of progress, and nobody will tell us anything," she said. "We're about ready to change doctors."

"You might find a better doctor," I said, "but wait a bit. Be patient. I'm sure your doctor is doing his best."

Then I told them about the time I reached the end of my patience:

"When my doctor came in to see me I was fuming.

"'Sit down!' I yelled.

"He did, and for maybe five minutes I complained about everything that bothered and upset me. As I watched his face, I realized I had hurt his feelings. I hadn't been thinking about him, of course. I was hurting, never pain free, couldn't sleep, and I wanted answers. 'I get tired of all this not knowing. I ask you how long I have to wear this, and you say, "Maybe another month, maybe two months, maybe three months."' I wasn't through yet, and my anger really burst out with another round of complaints. I ended with, 'Why can't you give me a straight answer?'

"He dropped his head and said softly, 'I'm doing the best I can. I don't know the answers. That's why I can't tell you.'

"'I'm just looking for—'

"'I know you are, but this isn't an exact science. We're re-inventing the wheel. We don't have that much experience in this area, and this is all new technology for us. We're doing the best we can.'"

After I told Brad and his wife about that incident, I added, "Please be patient with your doctor. He can't give you answers he doesn't have. He'll also tell you things to do and load you down with prescriptions. He's going to put you in a lot of therapy, and you're just going to have to learn how to deal with it—with all of it."

"Yeah, I know," he said, "but I just can't control my emotions anymore. I'm a cop. I've seen a lot of hard, bad, difficult stuff. I find myself just breaking down—I mean, real emotional. Know what I mean?"

"Absolutely. Just go ahead and break down. It'll happen again."

"I feel out of control."

"You are out of control!"

Brad stared at me.

"Think about it. What can you control? Nothing."

"I can't even wipe myself."

"That's right. You're totally helpless. There's nothing you can do or control."

"Before this I was a weight lifter and a bodybuilder," he said. "I had a physique you wouldn't believe."

"I have no doubt about that." I could see that he had once been muscular and strong. "But you don't have that now. You may have a great body again someday, but the inability to get up and do the things that you used to do will cause you to change. Be prepared to change. You're going to lose weight; muscles will atrophy. You can't control your body the way you did before."

His wife was obviously feeling all the stress as well, and she was on the verge of tears. "He just feels so bad, even with medication. I just don't know what to do."

"I can suggest a few things. First of all, manage the visits and phone calls. You don't have to let everyone come whenever they want," I said. "Be firm. If you allow everyone to come, you'll wear yourself out trying to be nice. Your friends will understand."

Then I turned to Brad. "Be prepared for all your therapy, because you're going to have to do all kinds of difficult things. Do them if you want to learn to walk again. Be patient, because it will take a long time. Probably one of the best things I can tell you is this: Don't try to act like the Lone Ranger." I paused briefly and almost smiled, because I remembered how I had been. "Let people know where you hurt and how they can help—especially the people you trust. Let them know so they can do things for you. Let them pray for you. You've got a lot of nice folks coming by here, and they want to bring you a cake, cook a meal, or do something for you. Let them express their friendship and love."

After I had talked a few minutes, I got up to leave. I wrote down my phone number. "Call me. If you're struggling to go to sleep at three o'clock in the morning or you're angry, call me. I'll listen. I'll understand because I *can* understand. It's a small fraternity, and none of us joined it by choice."

Before I left, Brad said, "I can't tell you how much I appreciate your coming by. Just visiting with somebody who knows about the pain helps me a lot. You're the first person I've met who understands what it's like to live with pain twenty-four hours a day."

"It's not something I set out to do—visiting people who are where I was," I said, "but I'm willing to do it. I want to help, but you're going to have to make the effort to call me. Remember—don't try to tough it out alone."

Brad's wife followed me out to the car and said, "He needed this. In public he tries to be the source of strength and sound positive. In quiet moments he's frustrated and emotional, and he falls apart. I've been really worried about him. Never in our lives together have I seen him this way."

"I remember my wife working hard all day teaching school and then coming to spend the evening with me," I said. "Just hang in with him. He will get better."

185

I told her that one time when I was at my worst, Eva had tried to encourage me and had said something like, "Just give it time. You're going to be fine."

I had exploded with frustration and rage—"What makes you think I'm going to be fine? What are the odds of my ever being fine? Nobody can ever tell me that. Nobody can promise me that."

To her credit, Eva hadn't argued. She'd wrapped her arms around me. I had wept. I had never done that before in her presence.

After I told that story to Brad's wife, I said, "Be prepared for changes in your life and his. He can't control his emotions, but don't take it as a personal attack when he yells or screams. It's the pain and the frustration, not you." I shook her hand and said, "And for goodness' sake, call me if you need me. Push Brad to call me."

After that, I saw Brad four or five times. Weeks later when he was able to get out of the house with his walker, I spotted him in a restaurant. I went over to his table and sat down. "How are you doing?" I asked.

"I'm doing okay. Really okay." He thanked me again for coming at one of his lowest moments. He still wasn't in top shape, but he was getting healthy again. When he clasped my hand and held it a long time, I knew it was his way of expressing his appreciation in ways he couldn't put into words.

I felt grateful to God for being able to help Brad in his dark time.

———

About two years after my accident, I heard that Chad Vowell had been in a serious car accident. He had been a member of our youth ministry at South Park, and his parents were among the most supportive parents I had at the church. His mother,

Carol, was on the committee that came to my hospital room with others to plan youth retreats. I hadn't been very helpful, but it had been their way of making me feel useful and needed.

Chad had been an outstanding soccer player and was with our youth group about a year before he went to college.

When I called his mother, she told me they had helicoptered Chad to John Sealy Hospital in Galveston. I had no idea just how serious he was until she added, "The report is that he has mangled his lower leg and is in a fixator."

When I heard the word *fixator*, I knew I had to see him. I would have gone anyway, because he was a member of South Park. But the word *fixator* gave extra urgency.

When I walked into his room, Chad lay there depressed, and he obviously didn't want to talk. This wasn't the Chad I knew. Before that, he'd always been glad to see me, and his face would light up in recognition. This time he acknowledged my presence but made no effort to engage in conversation.

"Are you okay? Are you going to be all right?" I asked and then looked at his leg. "I see they gave you a fixator."

"Yeah, they did," he said.

"Chad, you remember when I had my accident? That's the same thing they put on me."

"Really?" he asked. For the first time he looked at me with interest. I don't know if he'd never seen me with mine or if he just didn't remember. I leaned closer and said, "Just remember this: I know what it feels like to have one of them."

His injury was on the lower leg. Because there are two bones in the lower leg it's less difficult to heal. As I learned before I left, his prognosis was very good.

I was able to talk to that boy, hold his hand, and pray with him in a way that made him realize I identified with his plight. For the first time, he had a sense of what he had to look forward to in his treatment. Until then, like me after my accident, no one would give Chad any specific information. Like me, he felt angry and depressed.

"The pain will last a long time, and the recovery will seem to last forever, but you'll get better. Just remember that: You will get better."

And he did.

———

Cancer claimed Joyce Pentecost one week before her thirty-ninth birthday. I loved her very much. She was married to Eva's brother Eddie and left behind two beautiful redheaded kids, Jordan and Colton.

Not only was Joyce one of the liveliest people I've ever met, and a fireball of a singer, but she could also light up a room by merely entering it. She rarely just sang a song; she belted it in the great tradition of Ethel Merman.

I felt honored to speak at her memorial service at First Baptist Church of Forrest City, Arkansas. More than six hundred people packed the auditorium. Because Joyce had recorded several CDs of Christian music, she left a legacy for the rest of us. On that sunny afternoon, we heard Joyce sing her own benediction.

Following her recorded music, her father, Reverend Charles Bradley, delivered a message of hope and salvation. He told the crowd, "Years ago Joyce and I made a covenant. If I went first, she would sing at my funeral. And if she went first, I would speak at hers. Today I am fulfilling that promise to my baby girl."

That moment still stays with me. Melancholy smiles broke out, tears flowed, but I don't think anyone felt anger or hopelessness.

After Joyce's father concluded his message, it was my turn to speak.

"Some may ask today, 'How could Joyce die?'" I said. "But I would say to you the better question is, how did she live? She lived well, beloved. She lived very well."

I told the hurting throng that Joyce was a redheaded comet streaking across the stage of life, that she lived and loved to make people happy, that she was a devoted friend, an ideal daughter, a doting aunt, a sweet sister, a loving mother, and a wonderful wife. I admitted freely that I didn't have the answer to the question that must have penetrated many hearts in the room: Why?

"There is comfort when there are no answers," I said. "Joyce firmly believed that if she died, she would instantly be with God. She believed that if she lived, God would be with her. That was her reason for living. That can be our reason for carrying on."

I concluded by sharing one personal moment. The last extended conversation I had with Joyce before she returned home from the hospital was about heaven. She never tired of hearing me describe my trip to heaven, so we "visited" there one final time. We talked of the angels, the gate, and our loved ones. (Joyce's own mother had died of cancer.) Joyce always wanted me to describe the music, and our final conversation together was no different.

"Just a few days ago," I said to the congregation, "I believe God was sitting behind those gates, and he told the angels, 'What we need around here is a good redheaded soprano.'

"'That would be Joyce Pentecost!' the angels said.

"God sent for Joyce, and she answered the call. She is singing now with the angelic hosts. Joyce Pentecost is absent from the body but present with the Lord."

My final words at the service were a question: "Can you lose someone if you know where she is?"

I was thirty-eight years old when I was killed in that car wreck. Joyce was the same age when she was diagnosed with cancer. I survived the ordeal; Joyce did not. But I know this: Because I was able to experience heaven, I was able to prepare her and her loved ones for it. And now I am preparing you.

Many times since my accident I have wished someone who had already gone through the ordeal of wearing a fixator for months had visited me in the hospital. I know it would have relieved a lot of my anxiety.

Whenever I hear about people having a fixator, I try to contact them. When I talk to those facing long-term illness, I try to be totally honest. There is no easy way through that recovery process, and they need to know that. Because I have been there, I can tell them (and they listen) that although it will take a long time, eventually they will get better. I also talk to them about some of the short-term problems they'll face.

My visits with Chad and Brad and others also remind me that God still has a purpose for me on earth. During that long recovery period, I sometimes longed for heaven. Looking back, however, I can see how the personal experiences I have shared with others provided a gentle pull earthward when I was in heaven. "When God is ready to take me," I was finally able to say, "he'll release me." In the meantime, I try to offer as much comfort as possible to others.

Like me, when other victims first see the fixator attached to their leg, and especially when they begin to experience the pain and their inability to move, depression flows through them. They have no idea what's going to happen next. Even though doctors try to reassure them of recovery, they hurt too much to receive comfort from the doctors' words.

Sometimes, however, the patients may be inadvertently misled into saying to me, "I'll get over this soon."

"You may get over it, but it won't be soon," I say. "This is a long-term commitment, and there's no way to speed up the process. When you face injuries of this magnitude, there is no easy way out. You have to live with it for now."

I could share other stories, but these are the experiences that kept me going through some of my own dark periods. I found purpose again in being alive. I still long to return to heaven, but for now, this is where I belong. I am serving my purpose here on earth.

17

LONGING FOR HOME

You do this because you are looking forward to the joys of heaven—as you have been ever since you first heard the truth of the Good News.

Colossians 1:5

One of my favorite stories is about a little girl who left her house and her mother didn't know where she had gone. Once the mother missed her, she worried that something might have happened to her child. She stood on the front porch and yelled her daughter's name several times.

Almost immediately the little girl ran from the house next door. The mother hugged her, said she was worried, and finally asked, "Where have you been?"

"I went next door to be with Mr. Smith."

"Why were you over there?"

"His wife died and he is very sad."

"Oh, I'm so sorry, I didn't know that," the mother said. "What did you do?"

"I just helped him cry."

In a way, that's what I do. Sharing my experiences is my way of crying with others in pain.

～

I've discovered one reason I can bring comfort to people who are facing death themselves or have suffered the loss of a loved one: I've been there. I can give them every assurance that heaven is a place of unparalleled and indescribable joy.

Without the slightest doubt, I know heaven *is* real. It's more real than anything I've ever experienced in my life. I sometimes say, "Think of the worst thing that's ever happened to you, the best thing that's ever happened to you, and everything in between; heaven is more real than any of those things."

Since my return to earth, I've been acutely aware that all of us are on a pilgrimage. At the end of this life, wherever we go—heaven or hell—life will be more real than this one we're now living.

I never thought of that before my accident, of course. Heaven was a concept, something I believed in, but I didn't think about it often.

In the years since my accident, I've repeatedly thought of the last night Jesus was with his disciples before his betrayal and crucifixion. Only hours before he began that journey to heaven, he sat with his disciples in the upper room. He begged them not to be troubled and to trust in him. Then he told them he was going away and added, "In my Father's house are many rooms; if it were not so, I would have told you. I am going there to prepare a place for you. And if I go and prepare a place for you, I will come back and take you to be with me that you also may be where I am" (John 14:2–3 NIV).

I had never really noticed it before, but twice Jesus used the word *place*—a location. Perhaps that may not stir most people, but I think about it often. It is a literal place, and I can testify that I know that place. I've been there. I know heaven is real.

Since my accident, I've felt more intensely and deeply than ever before. A year in a hospital bed can do that for anyone, but it was more than just that. Those ninety minutes in heaven left such an impression on me that I can never be the same person I was. I can never again be totally content here, because I live in anticipation.

I experienced more pain than I thought a human could endure and still live to tell about it. In spite of all that happened to me during those months of unrelenting pain, I still feel the reality of heaven far, far more than the suffering I endured.

Because I am such a driven person and hardly ever slow down, I have often felt I needed to explain why I can't do certain things. When I'm fully dressed, most folks would never realize I have such debilitating injuries. However, when I face an activity that this reconstructed body just can't do (and people are sometimes surprised how simple some of those acts are), I often get strange responses.

"You look healthy," more than one person has said. "What's the matter with you?"

Occasionally, when I follow someone down a flight of stairs— a difficult experience for me—they hear my knees grinding and turn around. "Is that awful noise coming from you?" they ask.

"Yes." I smile and add, "Isn't it ridiculous?"

My relative mobility is quite deceptive. I get around better than anyone imagined I would. But I know—even if it doesn't show—that I'm quite limited in what I can do. I work hard to walk properly, because I don't want to attract attention to myself. I had enough stares and gawks when I wore my fixator.

Trying to act and look normal and to keep pushing myself is my way of dealing with my infirmities. I've learned that if I stay busy, especially by helping others, I don't think about my pain. In an odd way, my pain is its own therapy. I intend to go on until I can't go anymore.

We're such victims of our human invention of time that we have to think in temporal concepts—it's the way we're wired. That's an important point for me to make. My human inclination is to wonder what my welcoming committee is doing during these years while I'm back on earth.

As I ponder this, I don't believe my greeting committee said, "Oh no, he doesn't get to stay." They're still there at the gate. They're waiting. For them, time is not passing. Everything is in the eternal now—even if I can't put that into words. Even if ten more years pass, or thirty, in heaven it will be only an instant before I'm back there again.

Going to heaven that January morning wasn't my choice. The only choice in all of this is that one day I turned to Jesus Christ and accepted him as my Savior. Unworthy as I am, he allowed me to go to heaven, and I know the next time I go there, I'll stay.

I don't have a death wish. I'm not suicidal, but every day I think about going back. I long to return. In God's timing, I know with utter certainty that I will. Now I look forward to that time and eagerly await the moment. I have absolutely no fear of death. Why would I? There's nothing to fear—only joy to experience.

As I've pointed out before, when I became conscious again on earth, a bitter disappointment raged through me. I didn't want to return, but it wasn't my choice.

For a long time, I didn't accept that God had sent me back. But even in my disappointment, I knew that God had a purpose in everything that happened. There was a reason I went to heaven and a purpose in my returning. Eventually, I grasped that God had given me a special experience and a glimpse of what eternity will be.

Although I long for my heavenly home, I'm prepared to wait until the final summons comes for me.

Going through thirty-four surgeries and many years of pain has also helped me realize the truth of Paul's words to the Corinthians: "Praise be to the God and Father of our Lord Jesus Christ, the Father of compassion and the God of all comfort, who comforts us in all our troubles, so that we can comfort those in any trouble with the comfort we ourselves have received from God" (2 Cor. 1:3–4 NIV).

As long as I'm here on earth, God still has a purpose for me. Knowing that fact enables me to endure the pain and cope with my physical disabilities.

In my darkest moments, I remember a line from an old song: "It will be worth it all when we see Jesus."

I know it will.

18

The *Why* Questions

Now we see things imperfectly as in a poor mirror, but then we will see everything with perfect clarity. All that I know now is partial and incomplete, but then I will know everything completely, just as God knows me now.

1 Corinthians 13:12

Many times I've watched people on TV who say they've had near-death experiences (NDE). I confess to being fascinated, but I also admit to being skeptical. In fact, I'm highly skeptical. Before and after those people spoke, I thought, *They've probably had some kind of brain lapse. Or maybe there was already something in their memory bank and they just re-experienced it.* I didn't doubt their sincerity; they wanted to believe what they talked about.

I've watched many talk shows and read about victims who had died and been heroically resuscitated. Descriptions of their ordeals often seemed too rehearsed and disturbingly similar, as if one person copied the story of the last. One person who claimed to have been dead for more than twenty-four hours wrote a book and said he had talked to Adam and Eve. Some of the things the first earthly couple purportedly told him don't measure up with the Bible.

Despite my skepticism—even today—of many of their testimonies, I have never questioned my own death. In fact, it was so powerful, so life-changing, that I couldn't talk about it to anyone until David Gentiles pried out the information almost two years after the accident.

I have looked at the research on NDE and thought about it often during the years.

In December 2001, *Lancet*, the journal of the British Medical Society, reported research on NDE. Most scientific and medical experts had previously dismissed these dramatic occurrences as wishful thinking or the misguided musings of oxygen-starved brains.

The study, conducted in the Netherlands, is one of the first scientific studies. Instead of interviewing those who reported they had once had a NDE, they followed hundreds of patients who had been resuscitated after suffering clinical death—that is, after their hearts stopped. They hoped that approach would provide more accurate accounts by documenting the experiences as they happened, rather than basing them on recollections long after the event of resuscitation.

Their results: About 18 percent of the patients in the study spoke of recollection of the time in which they had been clinically dead. Between 8 and 12 percent reported the commonly accepted NDE experiences, such as seeing bright lights, going through a tunnel, or even crossing over into heaven and speaking with dead relatives and friends. The researchers concluded that afterlife experiences or NDE are merely "something we would all desperately like to believe is true."[1]

Conversely, other scholars made conclusions based on their study of 344 people (ages twenty-six to ninety-two) who had been resuscitated. Most of them were interviewed within five days of the experience. The researchers contacted those same people two years later and then eight years after the event.

Researchers discovered that the experiences didn't correlate with any of the measured psychological, physiological, or medical parameters—that is, the experiences were unrelated to processes in the dying brain. Most patients had excellent recall of the events, which, the researchers said, undermined the idea that the memories were false.

The most important thing to me is that those who had such experiences reported marked changes in their personalities. They lost their fear of death. They became more compassionate, giving, and loving.

The study really proved nothing about the reality of NDE. As had been the case before the studies, one group believed NDE were merely the psychological states of those dying; the other group maintained that hard evidence supported the validity of near-death occurrences, suggesting that scientists rethink theories that dismiss out-of-body experiences.

I have no intention of trying to solve this debate. I can only relate what happened to me. No matter what researchers may or may not try to tell me, I *know* I went to heaven.

I've devoted an immense amount of time to considering *why* it happened rather than *what* happened. I have reached only one solid conclusion: Before being killed in a car accident, I remained skeptical of near-death experiences. I simply didn't see how a person could die, go to heaven, and return to tell about it. I never doubted dying, the reality of heaven, or life after death. I doubted descriptions of near-death stories. These stories all seemed too rehearsed and sounded alike. Then I died, went to heaven, and returned. I can only tell what happened to me. Not for an instant have I ever thought it was merely a vision, some case of mental wires crossing, or the result of stories I'd heard. I *know* heaven is real. I have been there and come back.

It comes down to this: Until some mere mortal is dead for a lengthy period and subsequently returns to life with irrefutable evidence of an afterlife, near-death experiences will continue to be a matter of faith, or at the very least, conjecture. But then, as one of my friends would say, "What else is new?"

One time I shared my experiences with a large congregation that included my wife's parents, Eldon and Ethel Pentecost. They've been consistently supportive and made great sacrifices during my accident and lengthy recovery.

After the service, we went to their home. At one point, Eldon and I were alone, and he told me, "I was angry the first time you shared your story of your trip to heaven."

I had no idea he felt that way.

"You finished by saying you never wanted to come back to earth."

I just nodded in affirmation, not knowing where this was going.

"I didn't understand it then, but I've changed. Now when I hear you talk about heaven's beauty, I understand a little better why you'd willingly be separated from my daughter and grandkids for a while. You know—you really do know, don't you—that they'll join you someday?"

"Without a doubt," I said.

Eldon's revelation caught me off guard. He was right, of course. I had the distinct privilege of baptizing my own children and seeing my wife baptized as well. I knew that their professions of faith were authentic. By faith, I knew that they would be residents of heaven someday. Being separated from them had never crossed my mind while I was in heaven. People in heaven simply don't have an awareness of who is *not* there. They do know who is coming.

Even today, I can say honestly that I wish I could have stayed in heaven, but my ultimate time had not yet come. After leaving heaven, if I had known that I would face two weeks in ICU, a year in a hospital bed, and thirty-four operations, I surely would have been even more disheartened from the outset. However, this was not my choice, and I returned to the sounds of one voice praying, boots crunching glass underfoot, and the Jaws of Life ripping through my shattered auto.

One question keeps troubling me: *Why?* It takes many forms.

Why did I die in that car wreck?

Why did I have the unique privilege of going to heaven?

Why did I glimpse heaven, only to be sent back?

Why did I nearly die in the hospital?

Why has God let me live in constant pain since January 18, 1989?

The short answer: I don't know. And yet that single word, *why*, remains the consummate human query. By nature, we're curious. We want to know.

All these years later, it's still not easy for me to relate what happened. Several times I tried to write this myself but couldn't. That's why I asked my friend Cec Murphey to help me with this book—if it were up to me, this book would never have been written. The emotional trauma of reliving all the events is too difficult. Only with someone else actually writing it has it finally been possible to go through this ordeal.

I still don't know why such things happen.

I do know God is with me in the darkest moments of life.

Besides asking why, there are other questions. I think they're even more important for me to ponder.

Did God want me to know how real pain could feel so that I could understand the pain of others?

Did God want me to know how real heaven is?

What did God want me to learn from all my experiences, my death, and the long period of recovery?

How can my experiences be of the most benefit to others?

After all these years, I don't have the answers to most of those questions either. I have learned a few things and realize that God still has reasons for keeping me alive on earth. I may never know his reasons, and God has no obligation to explain them to me.

Even though I don't have full answers to many of my questions, I do have peace. I know I am where God wants me to be. I know I'm doing the work God has given me.

I find comfort in a story recorded in John's Gospel. A man born blind meets Jesus and is healed. After that, he runs around praising God, but his healing is an embarrassment to the religious leaders who have been trying to turn the people against Jesus. They interrogate the formerly blind man, trying to force him to admit that Jesus is a sinner (that is, a fraud).

The man wisely says, "Whether he is a sinner or not, I don't know. One thing I do know. I was blind but now I see!" (John 9:25 NIV). In the same way, some may not believe my account; they may think it was some kind of wish fulfillment during a point of severe trauma. I don't have to defend my experience.

I know what happened to me. For those of us whose faith is in the reality of heaven, no amount of evidence is necessary. *I know what I experienced.* ·

I believe God gave me a hint of what eternity in heaven will be like.

I also believe that part of the reason I am still alive, as I've already pointed out, is that people prayed. Dick Onerecker prayed me back to life—to live without brain damage. David

Gentiles and others prayed so that God wouldn't take me back to heaven just yet.

I am here, I am alive, and it's because God's purposes have not yet been fulfilled in my life. When God is finished with me, I'll return to the place I yearn to be. I have made my final reservation for heaven and I'm going back someday—permanently.

Prayerfully, I'll see you there too.

19

STORIES OF
ENCOURAGEMENT

When Don approached me to help him write the book that became *90 Minutes in Heaven*, I was extremely skeptical. I knew about near-death experiences and told him I wasn't interested in writing on that topic.

"I died," Don said. "I really died."

I smiled indulgently. Although I liked the man, I didn't believe him. I didn't doubt his sincerity, only his interpretation of the event.

Although Don could have found a dozen other writers, he pursued me. We emailed several times and talked by phone for about six weeks. Then Don said, "If my heart had been beating during that time, I would have bled to death." (There was no abnormal loss of blood from his accident.)

He pointed out several other facts to support his claim of having died, but one seemed especially significant. Four emergency medical technicians—four professionals—reported they could find no pulse. As Don reminded me, the human brain can't survive more than six minutes without severe brain damage.

That's when I became a believer in Don's experience.

Over the decade since the release of the book, many other individuals also became believers and fans. Don has received thousands of emails from people who have read *90 Minutes in Heaven*, and millions around the world have heard him speak.

Because he receives thousands of emails and letters, Don has been unable to respond to every contact. However, he keeps every piece of correspondence.

When our publisher decided to issue a new edition, our editor, Vicki Crumpton, asked about testimonies from people whom Don had encountered.

Of the thousands he could have chosen, those that follow are special and typical of the various ways Don Piper's life and story have impacted others. The first four stories come from Don's experiences traveling around the country, the others are drawn from among the thousands of people who write to him. With the permission of the email writers, we are printing a few of them in the pages that follow.

Cecil Murphey

You Never Know

In February 2013, I spoke at First Baptist Church of Deer Park, a suburb of Houston, Texas, a few miles from my home. The auditorium was packed with people and we had a highly charged, exciting service. I shared my message, called "Getting to Heaven."

Among the crowd was a father named Pat Thomas and his twenty-one-year-old daughter, Katie. Several people said my words greatly affected both of them, especially the dad.

A week later, Katie, a student at San Jacinto College, died in a two-car accident that also claimed the lives of two freshmen from Texas A&M University.

An article in the *Houston Chronicle* quoted a friend of hers as saying, "I saw Katie every Sunday morning at Deer Park First Baptist Church." Katie heard the message of salvation the Sunday before she died.

She learned how to get to heaven and she's there now.

Carla Cothran, a friend of our family, knows the family and attended the funeral.

This is her report:

On March 3, 2013, Katie Lynn Thomas died in a car accident in Houston, Texas. Her car collided with another car and three Texas A&M students were inside. Two of the students died instantly and a third, in critical condition, was rushed to an area hospital. He survived.

The week before Katie died, her father, Pat Thomas, asked Katie to go with him to hear Don Piper speak and she went. Don's story was very moving to both of them. Pat bought the book *90 Minutes in Heaven*, read it, and said he just couldn't put it down.

The church overflowed with people for Katie's funeral. During the service, Pat Thomas spoke about Katie and told humorous stories about her childhood.

Then Pat said, "God used someone to powerfully prepare me for what was about to happen." He told about the two of them going to hear Don Piper's talk.

"If you have not read Mr. Piper's book, please do so soon," he said. "You never know when your time may come or you'll lose someone you love."

He also said that Katie had tattooed on her back Hebrews 11:1: "Now faith is the substance of things hoped for, the evidence of things not seen" (KJV).

Meet Me at the Gate

I preached at Fellowship of San Antonio in December 2012, for the True Vineyard Rwanda ministry. At the end of my message, I offered an altar call and several responded.

Among those who came forward was a woman who was obviously emotional. I took her hand and asked what was on her heart.

"I knew I had to do something, and I couldn't stay in my seat any longer," she said.

"Have you ever trusted Christ as your Savior?"

She shook her head.

"Would you like to do that right now?"

"I believe I would," she said, and smiled.

I prayed for her. When I looked up, her son was standing beside her. I introduced myself to him and asked, "Did you know that your mom just gave her heart to Jesus, and someday she will go to live in heaven?"

"I want to be where she is," he replied with a tone of utter sincerity.

"Would you like to ask Jesus into your heart?"

"Yes, sir!"

And he did.

On March 3, 2013, nearly four months later, I was back in that church, and I signed copies of my books after the service. I looked up to see that same woman. This time she was beaming.

"It's me! Remember? I've been coming to Fellowship of San Antonio ever since that night in December. It's the best thing that has ever happened to me!"

I was delighted to sign my name in her book, and I wrote, "Meet me at the gate."

And I know she will.

Fred's Legacy

In 2007, Fred Winters, pastor of First Baptist Church in Maryville, Illinois, invited me to speak. I was unable to make my schedule fit with his, so we set it up for the far-off date of Sunday evening, April 26, 2009.

I never got to meet Fred.

About 8:15 on Sunday morning, March 8, 2009—less than six weeks before I was scheduled to speak—a man shot Fred Winters inside the church shortly after the worship service began. They rushed him to the hospital but he had died instantly.

When I learned about Fred's death, I was preaching in Hawaii. I called the Maryville church immediately. Because they were flooded with incoming calls, no one on the staff was able to talk with me; however, about an hour later, Cindy Carnes, the church's business administrator, called back. I expressed my profound condolences. "I will be all right if you want to postpone my coming—"

"No! We need you now more than ever and Fred wanted you to come," she said.

"I'll be there," I said. "Anything I can do for you in the meantime?"

"Pray for us; we've never buried a pastor before."

Something about the way she spoke and the words she spoke burned in my heart. Inside my head, I can still hear the pain and confusion in her voice.

When I arrived at the church on the evening of April 26, their parking lots were completely filled. I saw no vacant seats in the church sanctuary, which seated three thousand. The choir started the service; they wore red shirts and black pants.

"Fred Winters has to be smiling down on the congregation to witness what he sees here," I said during my message. I reminded them that Fred was in heaven because he had chosen to go there years earlier. "Heaven is a prepared place for prepared people." I talked to them about being ready for heaven.

Mark Jones, a minister at the church, said later to a reporter, "The twofold approach of having Don Piper talking about heaven and what Pastor Fred was experiencing brought incredible healing to our congregation."

Mark said something else that I liked: "Pastor Fred would have been thrilled about having all the people at that meeting, but I think he would have asked, 'Why didn't we buy more chairs?'"

Before the service, Fred's widow, Cindy, and their two daughters, Alysia and Cassidy, spoke to newspaper reporter Dan Brannan. Cindy said, "[Don Piper] wasn't surprised about our divine appointment and had an understanding that God is at work in our world and in our individual lives to reach out to us and reveal himself to us." She went on to say, "I felt a strong connection with [Don], because he brought us reassurance about Fred's complete joy and peace in heaven. This is something we knew, but to hear him express this sentiment in a real way, because he has experienced heaven, was like a warm blanket for our hearts."[1]

I'd like to tell you something I learned about Fred and Cindy. They married when she was eighteen and together they built a successful ministry at the Maryville church. On Saturday night before his death, Fred was home with the family. In Cindy's words, "That night, he and I were goofing off and laughing. In the midst of our joking around, he looked at me and said, 'You know, you are my best friend.'"

She smiled and they continued their bantering. But after his death, she said, "That is now a very precious moment to me. In the goofiness of the moment for him to have stopped and said those words is a gift from God. God knew I would need that."

Three weeks had passed before I spoke at the church, and she was still grieving her loss. She talked openly about Fred, whom she had known since she was fourteen years old. "I have a huge hole in my heart with him no longer here. There are moments I think about living the rest of my life without that connection. It's painful to think about that. I was looking forward to spending the rest of my life with somebody and the next day I don't have him anymore."

On the Sunday evening of the day Fred died, grief-stricken Cindy picked up *90 Minutes in Heaven*. Her husband had read the book two years earlier when he first contacted me. Several times he had mentioned the book to her, but she hadn't read it.

That night she read the first three chapters. "Chapters two and three brought me so much comfort and understanding," Cindy said. "I don't know how I would have made it through that night without knowing what Fred was experiencing in heaven."

She gave copies of my book to the police, firefighters, and emergency-room staff who had been involved that night. She invited all of them to First Baptist Church, and hundreds came in uniform the night I spoke.

Cindy had insisted that I still come to speak at the church. I'm so glad she did. She told me that she still reflects on the love and friendship she and Fred shared. She frequently quotes Romans 8:28, "And we know that in all things God works for the good to those who love him, who have been called according to his purpose" (NIV).

"That verse conveys Fred's perspective on life. No matter what happens, we can allow God to bring good out of this, even if it is evil," Cindy said. "That is what Fred would want us to do. I pray for the man who shot Fred and pray that he will find peace from God."

I also want to mention the results of the life and death of Fred Winters. Cindy and those at the church have received boxes of cards and letters. Mark Jones told me about an email from a college student, saying that, "The student from Alabama says he is praying for us every day." He reflected that this young man is probably around twenty, working on his degree with huge decisions ahead, and yet he is thinking of someone else.

One church compiled a message tribute called "You Are Not Alone," which let those at First Baptist in Maryville know they were standing by them and praying for them.

They've received messages from around the world, many of which weren't in English. The word spread and many people expressed their compassion. Most of them had the consistent theme that they were praying for Fred's family and the congregation.

Mark also said, "There's something encouraging and comforting in knowing that God has prompted Christians we'll probably never meet to pray for people in the middle of a cornfield in Illinois. We believe that those prayers are being offered up on our prayers and they are tremendously impacting our church in a positive way."

After I had been to the church, they posted these interesting facts on their website: the Sunday after my visit, 1,483 people attended church services. In the weeks after Fred's death, the church witnessed an increase of 278 people at Sunday services. Between March 8 and May 17, average church attendance grew by 210 people in the morning and 230 in the evening service, and morning Sunday school classes increased by 80. On Easter Sunday, 36 people professed faith in Jesus Christ and joined the church.

As I've reflected on that tragedy, I admit I don't understand—and no one does. But I believe God used Fred Winters not only in his life but also in his death to provide a powerful legacy and a greater reward in heaven.

One Father's Pain

"I had to come to this meeting. My daughter was murdered four weeks ago."

Those first two sentences certainly grabbed my attention.

I had preached a series in a church in Columbia, South Carolina. Afterward, I sat at a table to sign copies of my books. I like book signings because I get a chance to talk directly with people. And some of them have amazing stories to tell me.

As his words sunk in, I put down my pen and stared at him. "I'm sorry for your loss—"

That's as far as I got before he blurted out his story. Other people waited in line behind him, but I felt that father needed to tell me the full story.

"I went into horrible depression. My heart was broken," he said. "I couldn't accept her death, especially such a violent one." He wiped tears from his eyes before he continued. "I hardly ate anything. I lost weight. I couldn't sleep. As soon as I closed my eyes, my grief overwhelmed me. It didn't get better and my depression grew worse. Friends from my church insisted that I go to our family doctor. I resisted, but they came to my house and took me anyway."

His voice softened, and I leaned forward to hear the rest of his story.

"The doctor said I needed regular meals, rest, and recuperation. But I knew that much. He told me to take better care of myself, or I would die too. I told him I didn't care. But then he said, 'Yes, but your brothers and sisters from church do. They don't want another funeral!' And he phoned in a prescription for a tranquilizer and an appetite stimulant."

"And those helped?"

He held up his hand because he wanted to finish his story. "Right after that, my friends took me to the CVS pharmacy near our home to pick them up."

He told me he stood in line at the pharmacy, but he felt so weak from loss of sleep and little food, he became lightheaded and dizzy. "I felt myself starting to faint. Next to me was one of those bookracks and I grabbed it to break my fall.

212

"That was enough to brace me. In doing that, somehow I wrapped my hand around one of the books in the rack." He smiled and said that as he stood up he looked at the title of the book he had grabbed.

"It was *90 Minutes in Heaven*. And the word *heaven* seemed to jump out at me. I skimmed through the book and saw the chapter called 'New Normal' and I had to read it. I didn't care about the prescriptions or anything around me."

I smiled at him as he said, "I knew that was a divine appointment."

He held up his obviously well-read copy and asked me to sign it. As I wrote in it, he said, "Isn't God good? I went to the pharmacy to get a prescription to help me, and God put one right in front of my eyes."

I said, "Yes, God is good all the time!"

"I know where my daughter is right now. I can celebrate her life and have a meaningful life myself until God calls me home to be with her."

Email from Readers

An Ilizarov Club Member

I was your neighbor in St. Luke's Episcopal Hospital in 1989. Over the years I've had three more frames (fixators). The improvements have been good but it's still the most painful thing I've ever experienced. I enjoyed your book and have gotten a lot of comfort and joy from people locally and from church members who recognized me.

Despite many complications, I wore that first frame for almost two years. It was my doctor's first use of the Ilizarov frame. We finally just let me heal and he removed it without my getting all the length my leg needed. That's why, years later, I had to wear two more frames. I think it would be nice to hear from you because so few people (even those who went through it by our sides—my beautiful family and dedicated mom) truly understand what it feels like to experience THE ILIZAROV.

—Christy White

Another Raging Hypocrite

I have just finished reading your book, *90 Minutes in Heaven*. I feel compelled to drop you an email to express my heartfelt thanks for your testimony within its pages, as well as your continuing ministry of love for our God and our Lord Jesus Christ.

I was deeply moved by the message of confirmation the book brought to my personal beliefs of what is yet to come for our faithfulness to him. I shall recommend to my friends that they place this book on their must-read list.

I'm a retired minister of the United Church of Christ. While attending college, I began my ministry on the first Sunday of June, 1955, with two small Methodist churches in my home state of West Virginia.

I moved to Wisconsin to attend seminary, later switching to the U.C.C. denomination and serving various churches until my official retirement in 1995, as the result of various medical problems. However, I continued to do supply preaching and interim work until my complete retirement on March 27, 2013, again brought about by increased medical and mobility problems. I will confess that the past eighteen years have been the most fruitful of my entire fifty-seven years of ministry.

To return to your testimony of the mysteries of God's workings, you have not only inspired me anew but have given me answers to weaknesses I didn't recognize in all my years of serving our Lord.

Beginning at about page 94, I read (and felt) the loving rebuke you received from your eighty-year-old retired friend, Jay B.

Perkins. I became aware that you and I ministered with the same self-imposed restrictions: I didn't want anybody to do for me while I did everything possible for them.

I burst out in tears after I read that account. I'd had that same attitude for fifty-seven years and now (at eighty-one years of age) I finally realized my greatest weakness; I too was a "raging hypocrite." I too "needed to get my act together," and it isn't too late. As our pastor, Bob, told me, "The past is past." I realized (like you) that the very best is yet to come.

After I informed Pastor Bob that I was reluctantly going to "hang it up," he replied, "You're going to have to preach one more time so our congregation can hear you once more as they celebrate your years of ministry."

"No!" I said. Then Jay's words jumped off the pages of your book: "How deeply they love you . . . and it's the only thing they have to offer you, and you're taking that gift away from them. This is their ministry and you would be spoiling it."

It was, without any doubt, the greatest celebration of my fifty-seven years and there were more tears. Thanks be to God, to you, and to Jay for opening my eyes and heart.

Now I, like you, found the greatest peace I've ever known, and I'm completely ready to go home.

Again I thank you, Don, for your life, faith, and ministry, for the ministry and example of your good wife, Eva, and for the challenge given by Jay.

I'll see you in heaven.

—Jim Kennedy

I Thought I'd Better Read Your Book

Thanks again for coming and sharing your ministry with us at Holy Cross Church. It was an extraordinary event in the life of our church and the Spirit's presence was undeniable.

I'm not the sort that goes for stories by people who say they've been to heaven. I'm sure I had seen your book around, but probably just moved on quickly to something else because I wasn't interested. It was watching one of your messages on Vimeo—a video-sharing website—that made me a fan. I thought, This guy is just telling us what the writer to the Hebrews says (paraphrased), "Life is difficult, but God can see you through."

I thought, if I'm going to introduce this guy, I'd better read the book. As busy as I was, I purchased and read the book *90 Minutes in Heaven*. I enjoyed the book very much and it was a good message.

My favorite part, the part that has stuck with me, was where you tell about being down in the dumps about all the things you couldn't do physically anymore as a result of your injuries.

You wrote that you came across a story about a man who had lost his eyesight later in life. He too was going on about all the things he couldn't do anymore, until a friend said to him, "Get over it." And that same friend told him to make a list of all the things he could do. The exercise turned that man's life around. You did the same, and the exercise turned you around.

We all need to hear a message like that. It's not about what we can't do. It's about what we can do. And the things we can do far exceed the things we can't, if we'll just stop and think about it.

On a personal note, it was a distinct pleasure meeting you. What you suffered was immense. Others have suffered similar things, but such suffering is rare. As you said, you're no hero. But God had a plan to use you in a special way that never would have been possible without the context in which he prepared you for the ministry you now have.

May God continue to bless you and Eva, and may the Lord bless others through the ministry God is doing through you.

All the glory belongs to him. But even so, someone has to reply, "Here I am, Lord, send me." Thanks for answering the call.

—The Rev'd S. A. Thompson, Rector, Holy Cross Episcopal Church, Sugar Land, Texas

Because of 90 Minutes in Heaven

I was in a very dark place in my life before I read your book. I was even feeling suicidal. Your book saved my life.

Even though you were going through physical pain and I was going through emotional pain, when you talked about "a new normal," something about that grabbed hold of me. And it changed everything for me forever. That and your description of what heaven is like made me want to be with God now and forever.

I grew up with a schizophrenic mother and later I adopted a child with severe emotional problems. So I was in a world of hurt before reading your book. That is no longer true. My life is wonderful now. God is so wonderful to me, but I would not be here if it were not for your books.

—Debra Brandenburg

I Gave Away Your Book

On a drive from Michigan to Ohio to visit my ninety-year-old mother, I stopped for a leg stretch and glanced at the Choice Books rack at the rest stop. I'm always on the lookout for another quality book for Mom, whose days consist of reading and music in her country home.

90 Minutes in Heaven caught my eye and I bought it. I read it before passing it on to her. That was two years ago.

Yesterday, I bought my fourth copy of the smaller gift version and my eighth copy of the full paperback version. We keep giving our copies away!

One went to a friend whose husband was killed by a tree falling on him last summer.

Another copy went to a friend who did not know Jesus personally when she was diagnosed with terminal lung cancer. Now she knows him. Soon she will share in your experience, but for all eternity. When I visit her, I remind her, "Dear friend, do not be afraid of death."

Your story has enriched my life and that of my husband enormously. I shared a capsule version of your story in the eulogy I gave for my aunt's funeral last winter.

Thank you, first to God Almighty for his miracle in your life, and second, to you for sharing your miracle with the rest of us.

In giving her permission to print her email, Marilyn added:

I explored old emails and found several where I offered to give a book to people I believed would benefit from it. After all this time, I'm still recommending and supplying copies of the book.

God has used various methods to speak to his people over the centuries. I believe he chose to use Don's experience to speak to our generations in this period of time.

—Marilyn Smaka

I Tried to Die

I am in the midst of reading your book *90 Minutes in Heaven*. I found it an interesting journey. Because of my own journey, I could relate to many of the things you wrote during your recovery. When I was twenty years of age, I suffered from major depression and was suicidal. I tried to die: I threw myself in front of a truck and the wheels rolled over both legs, crushing one but not the other.

It was a miracle that I survived and that doctors were able to save my leg. Unlike you, however, I had no faith in God at the time—although others were praying for me.

Like you, I now truly believe God saved me for a reason—his reasons. Over a period of time, the accident was to lead me, through a series of incidents, to God and to helping others.

I am enjoying reading your book, and it has helped me to see how far I have gone in my life. In saying this, I can't take credit for what has happened because this is God's work and will. I have now changed as a person and my behavior is the kind I can now live with. I no longer struggle with depression (I hope you don't either). I am drug and alcohol free—another miracle—and I'm helping others through my church.

I am happy to hear how much God has worked in your life and your family. God has used something as horrific as your accident to impact many lives throughout the world. What an amazing God. On the topic of amazing is your family. How blessed you are to have such a strong, supportive, loving family.

Keep kicking goals for God and may God continue to bless you, your family, and fellow Christians.

—Kevin Fitz

I Am a Miracle

In 2012 I was involved in a major motor vehicle accident in Germany. My car, a small 2009 Ford, was struck just forward of the driver's door by a late-model Mercedes Benz traveling at a high rate of speed.

I was traveling slowly at the time of the accident. The other driver was allegedly intoxicated.

I suffered sixteen broken bones: right tibia, right fibula, left femur, left humerus (in two places), left clavicle, sternum, ten ribs, and a dislocated left shoulder. I entered a German hospital in hemorrhagic shock and respiratory arrest.

The doctors tell us they believed I was in my last hour of life.

I have had nine surgeries, received 134 units of blood, and I've just completed sub-acute physical and occupational therapy, and will be evaluated this Friday. Next Monday I'll be evaluated for acute physical/occupational therapy.

I just finished reading *90 Minutes in Heaven*, and I received a huge blessing from your book. You hit the nail on the head in describing exactly how I felt during my treatment/recovery. I was in a total of four different medical facilities between July 21 and January 25. I was in a coma and then a drug-induced coma until I awoke on September 5, 2012.

Like you, I had difficulty letting people do things for me. The story you told of the motorcycle officer and his difficulties in controlling his emotions hit home because I was involved in law enforcement for more than twenty-five years.

I too had difficulty in my lack of control; especially when it came to bedpans and nurse's aides, young enough to be my children, taking care of those very private matters.

I have only spotty memories of June. I sang at the wedding of the daughter of a close friend, but I have no memory of that event. I don't have any memory of the accident or, for that matter, 99 percent of July 2012.

I simply woke up and was told about the accident. I assumed they told me the next day following the July 21 accident. I was wrong—it was September 5. I didn't get to see heaven while I was in the coma. I just woke up.

I'm writing to thank you for writing *90 Minutes in Heaven*. I've asked my wife, Shirley, to read it. Until I read your book, I believed the experiences you talked about during your recovery were unique to me. I am so glad to see they are not.

Shirley, who like Eva works full time, was and still is by my side, faithfully and lovingly caring for me. We married in 1975. Our children are grown and have lives of their own. I can never repay her.

My favorite chapter in the book was "The New Normal." I'd written on my Facebook page to my friends (before I read your book) that I was getting used to my new normal.

I look at my experience with this accident (still in litigation) as my own road to Damascus. I was very good at "talking the talk" but not at all good at "walking the walk."

While I don't believe it was God's will that I was involved in the accident (I'm a guitar/piano/drum player. There's not much left of my left arm or hand, and I'm having to learn to play guitar left-handed), I do believe God has something special planned for me. I am open, but all I feel God telling me right now is, "Just get better. Then we'll talk."

I am working on rehab. The test my neurologist did to find out what nerves in my left arm and left hand were damaged was the most painful ordeal I have had to endure. I was awake and no numbing medicine could be given. The result was disappointing. It looks as if I may not recover full use of my left arm or left hand.

I have forgiven the other driver. I know God allowed me to live. Like you, I had thousands (thanks to the internet) following my case and praying for me.

Through your book, I felt God reassure me and remind me that no matter how bad my pain is, it was nothing compared to his Son's agony for me.

Thank you. God bless your socks off.

—Dave Disch

Eight months after the accident, Dave emailed:

I felt led to write to Mr. Piper and I freely share my account with many, especially those who tell me I'm lucky or fortunate to be alive. I tell them, "No, I'm a miracle. I don't know why God allowed me this miracle but I'm going to live it the best I can."

I am in acute physical/occupational therapy now. My occupational therapist believes the nerves in my arm and hand are "waking up." While it's still too soon to be sure, she is cautiously optimistic of my chances of getting my hand back working one day. I can make a fist, and I can extend my fingers side to side and make the okay sign. And I have returned to work.

Zach Is Waiting

I'm writing to thank you from the bottom of my heart for sharing your story about what heaven is like.

Our fourteen-year-old son, Zack, died last Easter, very unexpectedly, in our home from an undiagnosed heart condition. Your book has put my mind at ease about what he experienced. From your description I know in my heart that my grandfather picked him up and swung him around as soon as he got there.

Thank you for sharing your story with the rest of us, and giving us hope for the afterlife. And I so look forward for my time to be there. I know Zack will be waiting there to wrestle with me when I arrive.

—Mike Gallaway

I Knew Where She Would Be

I'm a junior at Porter High School in Porter, Texas. I have just completed reading your book *90 Minutes in Heaven*. Over and over again I've read the chapters where you explain heaven. I just can't seem to get enough. That part of the book just blows my mind.

Your book and your experience have helped me have a better understanding of heaven. It also answered many questions. I am so overwhelmingly excited to have this reassurance.

I'd heard about your book, but never felt the need to read it. But one day, my mother came home with your book and told me the short version about how you died, went to heaven, and came back to life.

One morning, I woke up and felt curious to read your story. I started and stopped after you explained heaven. Shortly after I read that part, my great grandmother died. I loved her so much, but at her funeral I never cried. I was sad, but at the same time, I knew where she would be. She will now be one of the people to greet me in heaven when my time comes to leave the earth.

Eventually I finished your book, and it has actually helped me through some of my hardships in life.

—Jamie Henk

Relying on Others

This past Christmas, a friend gave me a copy of your book and asked me to read it. I will admit I am not a leisure reader, so it usually takes a topic that interests me. After getting the book, I got the bright idea that my church's small group should review the book. I belong to a small group that meets every Monday for an hour. We do everything from watching a video from Rob Bell, to reading a book, chapter by chapter, such as Blue Like Jazz or The Shack. This leads to some very interesting discussions.

We started the book January 19, 2009—twenty years and one day from the day you were in heaven. To add some more irony, I am currently thirty-eight years old and named Don.

I guess you could say I was able to identify with you from page 1, and I feel as if I have a strong understanding of your thought processes.

December 5, 1992, while in college, I had trouble viewing the chalkboard, so I called my mom, who immediately contacted my eye doctor. She made me make an appointment for that day. I reluctantly drove from Wheeling Jesuit University in

West Virginia, to Canonsburg, Pennsylvania, and went to my eye doctor.

Once there, he told me the troubling news that I had a detached retina and I needed to see a specialist immediately. To make a long story short, within ten hours I went from a happy college student five months from graduation to being on an operating table, and being told I would never see the same and might even become blind.

My surgery kept me in the hospital for a few days. My eye matted shut every night from the leaking blood. In the mornings, I couldn't open it on my own. My mom used saline to clean it out so I could open it. The white of my eye, I was told, looked like a piece of red meat. To make matters worse, they decided two days before Christmas to have my other eye done as a precaution, since it looked degenerative.

Detached retinas typically affect only the elderly, yet here I was, a healthy twenty-two-year-old, going through it. I asked specialists and others why it happened. Medically they had no answers.

I felt devastated during my recovery, because I was told I wouldn't be able to lift more than twenty pounds for a long time, and my vision would improve but never go back to correctable 20/20.

After many eye doctor visits and the passing of time, my vision improved to where I no longer see shadows. I am back to correctable 20/20 vision through contacts. Additionally, I graduated college and have become a successful businessman.

During my ordeal, I mostly thought of things I could no longer do. Being an athlete my whole life, it was hard to face the reality that I wouldn't be able to play sports the same as I did before. But after graduating from college in 1994, I answered an ad for adult baseball federation league tryouts. Not only did I play in the league, but I did so for ten years straight.

Unlike you, I was able to just about do everything I had done before, but still I could never accept aging, growing, and no longer being physically the person I used to be—until I read your book.

My church group loved it and I have passed it on to another friend. I know it wasn't easy sharing it with the world. I know you would have preferred not to do that, but had you not, many lives wouldn't have been touched the way your hand was held that very day. Thank you.

—Don Tiger

In giving his permission for us to use his email, Don added this:

I hope you use my story, not for me, but for my mom. I think one of the hardest things through my ordeal—and I think Mr. Piper's—was having to rely on others. I can't imagine what it was like for my mom to have to "baby" a twenty-two-year-old son. I think you raise your kids from infancy, changing diapers, dressing, and nurturing, and you don't think you will need to redo that all again, eighteen years later.

I remember her putting me in her bed to sleep because it was on the first floor, and she was there every morning when I woke. She stayed strong though I realize now that she was likely deeply scared that her son, who had been an athlete, excelled in school, and was getting ready to tackle the world was back to not being able to see and needed care like an infant.

The Lord Has a Purpose for Me

Your book blessed me beyond measure and gave me closure to my mother's passing in November.

We were best friends, and I was holding her in my arms when she took her last breath. I am a heart-failure patient, diagnosed at age thirty-five, and I'm now forty. My doctor at Vanderbilt told me I would probably live to my fifties.

I was so consumed with how unfair things were that I felt depressed all the time. For eighteen months, I stayed with my mother almost every day as she fought two types of primary cancer, while I was struggling to complete my PhD. I had so many questions about life and death and wondered what good it did to have a PhD and keep living when she wasn't here anymore.

After she passed, there were so many times I wanted to be with her and thought I couldn't live another day.

I've been a Christian since I was sixteen. My mother told me she was ready to go many times during her illness and that she didn't want me to worry about her. She said I needed to keep living my life regardless of what happened, and that God would not take her before he saw fit to do so.

Recently I was at the library, checking out several books on grief, and the librarian looked up and asked me if I had read *90 Minutes in Heaven*. We got into a discussion of heaven and the death of people close to us. I told her what I was struggling with. I checked out your book and started reading it last night. Without a doubt, I can say I am so happy that my precious mama is now in perfect peace and with our Lord.

I believe the Lord has a purpose for me and that like Mama said, and you also echoed, "God will not take us before it is time and we have served our purpose." The issue isn't about the duration of our life, but the contributions we make and those whom we touch. I am more convinced of that than ever.

I thank God for you and for your message. It does give life purpose knowing that she knows I will be there one day and that I have so much to look forward to. I also believe our Lord puts people in our lives at the right time. I have shared your book with several people and hope it touches them the way it touched me.

—Sharon M. Hutton

They're Not Applauding for You

My favorite part of your book was in the chapter called "Back to Church." You described the ordeal of getting into a wheelchair to attend church for the first time after your accident. Everyone was so happy to see you and wanted to touch you.

You mentioned they wheeled you up to the front of the sanctuary and asked you to speak. Before you could think of what to say, everyone started clapping and applauding.

Just then, God whispered to you, They're not applauding for you. You realized they were glorifying God.

You said only four words to the crowd: "You prayed, I'm here."

That part made me break into tears. I had to read it several times.

I suffer from bipolar disorder, which often leaves me with great anxiety about holding a job and affects my sense of self-worth. I've experienced periods of depression that are accompanied by suicidal thoughts and it's hard for me to bear. Yet I have been told that many people pray for me on a daily basis, even though I, myself, don't lift anyone else up in prayer.

When I read this portion of your book, I realized that when God heals me of bipolar disorder, people will applaud in the same way, and they will be glorifying God. It won't be because of anything I've done, but because God has proven faithful and restored me to my right mind—by answering their prayers. God will have done it all.

God is working quite powerfully in my life. I haven't suffered gracefully, and I'm not explaining myself well, but in reading that part of your book, your simple words resonated with me and gave me hope.

—Jim Bures

She's with Her Loved Ones Now

I've often wondered if dead people could see their own funeral or, as they say, keep an eye on their loved ones here on earth. After reading your account of meeting loved ones and friends in heaven, I'm more certain that after we die, we don't think about what we leave behind.

I recently lost my wife of forty-three years. She suffered from so many diseases, including cancer, that I think a medical textbook could be written about her. I know now that she isn't sleeping in her grave or suffering in her old body. She's present with all of her departed loved ones, including a child we lost during the early stages of pregnancy.

I'm a Christian singer-songwriter and an author. Many times I've experienced the death of friends and family members, but this loss hurts the most.

My wife would have identified with your pain and suffering even though hers wasn't anything like what you went through.

I don't understand all of God's ways, but I know he does all things for the glory of his kingdom. We belong to that kingdom, so it will be joy unspeakable when we get there.

—Joseph Roth

To End It All

When I was thirteen years old, my life turned upside down. My dad was (and still is) an alcoholic and came home drunk just about every night. He accused my mom of doing things wrong—which she hadn't. He said it was always her fault that things didn't go right.

I became depressed. And it grew worse. I felt as if I were inside a dark hole that I couldn't get out of. I sensed God's light and his trying to reach out to me. I felt so worthless, I couldn't respond.

My life continued to go downhill. I began cutting myself, but I didn't feel any better. Then I took all kinds of pills to end it all. Although I tried suicide several times, every single time it failed. My depression became so bad, I didn't know who I was anymore and my friends couldn't understand the change that had come over me.

In 2010, when I was seventeen years old, I came home one afternoon. I was so exhausted, I flopped on the bed. I just wanted to end it all. I felt I had no reason to live.

Then something happened. I can say it only like this: something moved inside me and I felt I had to go to my closet. There, on the floor, was a copy of *90 Minutes in Heaven*. Although I was unsure why, I picked it up and began to read. I read and I cried and kept on reading.

God used you to wake me up.

I felt God whisper, I want you to experience this, but not yet. I have something for you to do for me first.

My depression lifted and I knew I was different—more like my old self, only happier. And at peace. I began reading the Bible and listening to Christian music.

For the past three years, I've been clean and free from self-harm and suicidal thoughts. I can tell you that I've never felt closer to God than I do now. I no longer want to end it all.

I just wanted to say thank you to the man who inspired me to take that first step toward a relationship with God. Your book was literally a lifesaver.

—Hannah Haines

Letters from the Gulf

Not long after *90 Minutes* came out, I started hearing from military personnel serving in Iraq and Afghanistan, as well as their family members. By early January 2010, I had received 687 such emails. Their stories of faith, sacrifice, and loss touched me. I was moved that God would use my simple message to change their lives.

Here are a few samples.

—

I'm a National Guard soldier from the state of Alabama. My unit and I are currently on deployment in Iraq. We have been away from home since the summer of 2006. I got the chance to go home for two weeks in early March of last year. While at home, my wife introduced me to your book. I have been a Christian for years, and my wife is also a follower of Christ.

She told me how good your book was, so I decided to pick it up at a bookstore. After returning to Iraq, I started to read *90 Minutes in Heaven*, and I must say that this book is an incredible story. I couldn't put it down.

I wanted to let you know how inspirational your story is to someone who is already a believer. It gave me great reassurance about heaven. Not to say I didn't already believe how wonderful it will be, but your book bolstered my willingness to get there someday and sit with the Father.

I can't possibly imagine what pain you must have gone through, both physical and mental, or what strain that must have put on your family. What you did, to keep fighting to stay alive, and to be able to share this incredible story takes more guts than I could ever have.

Through reading your book, I know God has a plan for you and your life and ministry. I'm glad you're alive today to tell your story. I want to let you know how inspirational your story has been to me, and that it has strengthened my faith. I know that one day I will go to the great heaven where you went.

Thank you for sharing your story so that people like me can be inspired to become better Christians.

Over here in the army, we face many temptations to sin, but your story has strengthened my willingness to live harder for God, to do whatever I can to praise him, and share not only his story, but also yours. Sometimes it takes miracles to get people to believe.

I'm sure the miracle you experienced will influence many to come to know Christ. You have done so much, and I wanted to thank you for it.

—

I wanted to thank you for writing your inspirational book. Our son died in Iraq, in October 2005, while serving with the Marine Corps. We are Christians and through prayer and the love and support of so many, we've been able to accept his death and know that he's safe and happy in heaven.

Throughout this journey, I often wondered if I had faith enough to get me through the sorrow and I often asked why.

We saw God's work through the life of our son, and his death has led us to educate youth in the price of freedom. We have established a memorial fund to send students to Arlington Cemetery each year. The response from those trips has been remarkable. God is great and I found deep comfort in reading your book. Thank you and God bless you for your work.

—Nancy Szwydek, Warfordsburg, PA

—

I wanted to write and thank you for putting your experience into words in *90 Minutes in Heaven*.

My only child was killed in Iraq in March. He was only twenty-five. I was a single mother. When I found myself pregnant and unmarried, I thought my family would disown me. I should have known better because they're devout Christians (my mom's dad was a Baptist minister).

They didn't disown me, and I came to realize very quickly that my son was God's gift to me. Having that child turned my life around. He was the light of my life.

Since my son's death I have had many people tell me how strong I am. I've explained that I know God has a plan in this; because I don't understand the plan doesn't mean it doesn't exist.

Even though I know better, at night when it's quiet I've found myself questioning a lot of things. For example, I've questioned the existence of heaven. What if it's something we humans say exists to make the hurts in this world go away? What if when we die, that's all there is? Maybe I should have been ashamed to think that way, but the pain and the grief took over my thoughts.

Last week, I finally went to the bookstore. I'm not the only mother who ever lost her child and I figured that maybe I needed to get some self-help book to guide me through the journey. As I looked at the books in the self-help section, I didn't feel compelled to purchase any of them. Then I went to the religious section and found *90 Minutes in Heaven*.

Last night, I read it straight through. Thank you so much because I needed that message. I needed to believe that one day I would see my baby again. I'll see him whole and he'll be singing and welcoming me and I'll once again feel his hugs. My journey through this isn't over, but I'm deeply indebted to you for putting *your journey* into words.

My son died in Iraq in the summer of 2005.

The week of his funeral I saw your book *90 Minutes in Heaven*. I read the first part of it while I was still inside the store. I didn't buy it: I was probably still in shock.

I don't remember much about that day, but I remembered the title and I wanted to read it when I was ready. Two months later, I bought the book and read it in its entirety. It comforted me as

I continued to struggle with the loss of a great son. I wondered what he was experiencing.

My son and I had a special talk before he left. He was a Christian and possibly the best and bravest person I've ever known. He knew he might die but said, "If we don't fight the terrorists over there we'll be fighting them here at home."

Perhaps you can understand why I read the book again a month ago and then passed it to a woman who struggled with her own loss. She has since told me that it helped her.

Today I was in an airport and found your new book, *Daily Devotions Inspired by 90 Minutes in Heaven.* The story of the soldier who died in Iraq touched me: someone read *90 Minutes in Heaven* to him as he lay dying.

I read that story just before I watched several military members getting ready to board a plane for who knows where. My husband is an officer in the Ohio National Guard. He had returned from Afghanistan just before my son left for Iraq.

God has given you a special ministry. There are many grieving people in this world, and at this time, many new Gold Star families (those who have lost someone serving in the military). At times, the grief is overwhelming. We went from having a happy, healthy son to being lost without him. It's a comfort to know that this life is only temporary and eternal life with our Savior (and my son) is coming.

I had to write you. This week I finished reading *90 Minutes in Heaven.* I know you've heard this again and again, but I have to thank you from the bottom of my heart for writing the book.

We lost our marine son in Iraq in 2004. He was nineteen years old. My husband and I are believers.

Deep down I've known our son is in a better place. Despite that, I still continued to wonder if he is truly happy now.

The day our son left home before being deployed to Iraq, he and I were in the kitchen. He looked at me and said, "I worry about you and Dad and how you'll be if something happens to me."

I hugged him and said, "Don't worry about us; we'll be fine. You take care of yourself and come home." Whenever we heard from him while he was in Iraq, he wanted to make sure we were all right. He would tell us he was praying for us. Imagine that! He was the one in danger, but he thought of us.

Because of his attitude and concern, I wondered if he was sad because we had to endure this tragedy. After reading your description of heaven, I'm convinced he is now happy and enjoying eternity in the presence of God and everyone that knew and loved him.

I have bought and been given numerous books on death and mourning, and everything that goes along with losing a child. I've never been able to finish a single one. I started them but couldn't continue with them because they made me too sad. *Your book is the first book I have finished* and I couldn't put it down. I wished your description of heaven could have gone on and on.

In the years since we have lost our son, I've met several people who have lost children and have recommended your book to all of them and pray they will find the comfort I did.

Your story is truly heartwarming and inspiring, and I admire you for your strength and courage and, despite all your medical issues, the selfless act of sharing your experience with others. I will be praying for you.

Without the love and grace of God and my promise to Nick that we would be fine, we wouldn't have survived our loss. Thank you from the bottom of my heart for bringing me the peace of knowing Nick is truly happy now.

My name is Bobbie Samme. I read *90 Minutes in Heaven* and *Heaven Is Real*. Every night before bed I read from *Daily Devotions Inspired by 90 Minutes in Heaven*. I'm deeply comforted by your experience and by your words.

My beloved son, Lance Corporal Eric A. Palmisano, USMC, was killed in Iraq on April 2, 2006. He was my youngest son; he was only twenty-seven when he died. He was a brave, excellent marine and we're proud of him. If you Google Eric A. Palmisano, you will be able to read all about him and the words of those of us who loved him.

I'm writing to you because the two-year anniversary of Eric's passing over to the other side is this Wednesday, April 2, and after I finished reading *Heaven Is Real* (and rereading *90 Minutes in Heaven*) I felt compelled to write to you.

I know my son is happy and at peace now, but I still miss him very much. He was a loving, attentive son and he brought me many hours of happiness and wonderful memories. I'll reflect on those memories all this week, all the while missing him so badly that my heart aches.

Thank you so much for sharing your story with everyone. Like millions of others, I've found *great* comfort and peace as I mourn the loss of my beloved son, Eric.

May God's peace and strength be with you and allow you to continue your amazing ministry.

—Bobbie Samme, very proud marine mother
of Lcpl Eric A. Palmisano, USMC,
KIA Iraq 4.2.06.

I'm sure you've heard it before, but I wanted to let you know I finished your book, *90 Minutes in Heaven*, and enjoyed it. My son was killed in Iraq in January 2008, in a house rigged with an IED. Five other soldiers lost their lives that day.

I've always believed in heaven but as I am sure you have heard millions of times, I needed reassurance that my son was all right. He left a wife and two children.

I hoped he wasn't too sad leaving us all. It helped that you spoke of having no regrets while you were in heaven. I know this has all been said to you before but I felt the need to tell you again: Thank you for sharing your story.

MY FAVORITE
BIBLE VERSES AND
QUOTATIONS

My Favorite Bible Verses about Prayer

> But I would seek God's help
> and present my case to him.
> He does great things that we cannot understand
> and miracles that we cannot count.
>
> Job 5:8–9 GW

> It would be unthinkable for me to sin against the LORD by failing to pray for you. I will go on teaching you the way that is good and right.
>
> 1 Samuel 12:23 GW

> Know that the LORD singles out godly people
> for himself.
> The LORD hears me when I call to him.
>
> Psalm 4:3 GW

237

Before they call, I will answer.
While they're still speaking, I will hear.

Isaiah 65:24 GW

When you pray, don't ramble like heathens who think they'll be heard if they talk a lot. Don't be like them. Your Father knows what you need before you ask him.

Matthew 6:7–8 GW

At the same time the Spirit also helps us in our weakness, because we don't know how to pray for what we need. But the Spirit intercedes along with our groans that cannot be expressed in words. The one who searches our hearts knows what the Spirit has in mind. The Spirit intercedes for God's people the way God wants him to.

Romans 8:26–27 GW

I will do anything you ask the Father in my name so that the Father will be given glory because of the Son. If you ask me to do something, I will do it.

John 14:13–14 GW

If any of you needs wisdom to know what you should do, you should ask God, and he will give it to you. God is generous to everyone and doesn't find fault with them. When you ask for something, don't have any doubts. A person who has doubts is like a wave that is blown by the wind and tossed by the sea. A person who has doubts shouldn't expect to receive anything from the Lord. A person who has doubts is thinking about two different things at the same time and can't make up his mind about anything.

James 1:5–8 GW

Never stop praying. Whatever happens, give thanks, because it is God's will in Christ Jesus that you do this.

1 Thessalonians 5:17–18 GW

My Favorite Quotations about Prayer

Don't pray for tasks equal to your powers; pray for power equal to your tasks. —Phillips Brooks

Whatsoever we beg of God, let us also work for it. —Jeremy Taylor

Is your prayer a monologue or a conversation? —Anonymous

Pray for a tough hide and a tender heart. —Ruth Graham

Go to prayer and listen. —J. C. Macaulay

Practical prayer is harder on the soles of your shoes than the knees of your trousers. —Austin O'Malley

Pray to God, but continue to row to the shore. —Unknown

Prayer, among sane people, has never superseded practical efforts to secure the desired results. —Santayana

The man who says his prayers at night is a captain posting his sentinels. He can sleep. —Baudelaire

Don't pray when it rains if you don't pray when the sun shines. —Satchel Paige

My Favorite Bible Verses about Comfort

> Even if my father and mother abandon me,
>   the Lord will take care of me. . . .
> Wait with hope for the Lord.
> Be strong, and let your heart be courageous.
> Yes, wait with hope for the Lord.
>
>   Psalm 27:10, 14 GW

When he falls, he will not be thrown down headfirst
    because the LORD holds on to his hand.

> Psalm 37:24 GW

The victory for righteous people comes from the LORD.
    He is their fortress in times of trouble.

> Psalm 37:39 GW

God is our refuge and strength,
    an ever-present help in times of trouble.
That is why we are not afraid
    even when the earth quakes
    or the mountains topple into the depths of the sea.
Water roars and foams,
    and mountains shake at the surging waves.

> Psalm 46:1–3 GW

Sing with joy, you heavens!
Rejoice, you earth!
Break into shouts of joy, you mountains!
    The LORD has comforted his people
    and will have compassion on his humble people.

> Isaiah 49:13 GW

I will ask the Father, and he will give you another helper who
will be with you forever. . . . I will not leave you all alone. I will
come back to you.

> John 14:16, 18 GW

Good will and peace from God our Father and the Lord Jesus
Christ are yours! I always thank God for you because Christ
Jesus has shown you God's good will.

> 1 Corinthians 1:3–4 GW

We always thank God for all of you as we remember you in our prayers. In the presence of our God and Father, we never forget that your faith is active, your love is working hard, and your confidence in our Lord Jesus Christ is enduring.

1 Thessalonians 1:2–3 GW

Brothers and sisters, we don't want you to be ignorant about those who have died. We don't want you to grieve like other people who have no hope. We believe that Jesus died and came back to life. We also believe that, through Jesus, God will bring back those who have died. They will come back with Jesus. We are telling you what the Lord taught. We who are still alive when the Lord comes will not go into his kingdom ahead of those who have already died. The Lord will come from heaven with a command, with the voice of the archangel, and with the trumpet call of God. First, the dead who believed in Christ will come back to life. Then, together with them, we who are still alive will be taken in the clouds to meet the Lord in the air. In this way we will always be with the Lord.

1 Thessalonians 4:13–17 GW

We understand what love is when we realize that Christ gave his life for us. That means we must give our lives for other believers. Now, suppose a person has enough to live on and notices another believer in need. How can God's love be in that person if he doesn't bother to help the other believer?

1 John 3:16–17 GW

He will wipe every tear from their eyes. There won't be any more death. There won't be any grief, crying, or pain, because the first things have disappeared.

Revelation 21:4 GW

My Favorite Quotations about Comfort

The dew of compassion is a tear. —Lord Byron

It takes a true believer to be compassionate. No greater burden can be borne by an individual than to know that no one cares or understands. —Arthur Stainback

Biblical orthodoxy without compassion is surely the ugliest thing in the world. —Francis Schaeffer

Christianity demands a level of caring that transcends human inclination. —Erwin Lutzer

Ten rules for overcoming the blues: Go out and do something for someone else and repeat it nine times. —Anonymous

Job responds (to the destruction of his family and wealth), even before his health and wealth are restored by saying, "All of this is too wonderful for me." Job found contentment and even joy, outside the context of comfort, health and stability. He understood the story was not about him, and he cared more about the story than he did about himself. —Donald Miller[1]

My Favorite Bible Verses about Heaven

The heavens declare the glory of God,
and the sky displays what his hands have made.

Psalm 19:1 GW

Turn to God and change the way you think and act, because the kingdom of heaven is near.

Matthew 3:2 GW

I give them eternal life. They will never be lost, and no one will tear them away from me.

John 10:28 GW

In our present tent-like existence we sigh, since we long to put on the house we will have in heaven.

2 Corinthians 5:2 GW

We, however, are citizens of heaven. We look forward to the Lord Jesus Christ coming from heaven as our Savior. Through his power to bring everything under his authority, he will change our humble bodies and make them like his glorified body.

Philippians 3:20–21 GW

There will no longer be any curse. The throne of God and the lamb will be in the city. His servants will worship him and see his face. His name will be on their foreheads. There will be no more night, and they will not need any light from lamps or the sun because the Lord God will shine on them. They will rule as kings forever and ever.

Revelation 22:3–5 GW

My Favorite Quotations about Heaven

Can you tell a plain man the road to heaven? Certainly, turn at once to the right, then go straight forward. —William Wilberforce

Everybody wants to go to heaven, but nobody wants to die. —Joe Louis (When the Piper family visited Arlington National Cemetery, among many famous folks' burial plots we saw former heavyweight boxing champion and US Army veteran Joe Louis's grave. I remember seeing this favorite quote of mine when we passed his grave.)

Has the world been so kind that you should leave the world with regret? There are better things ahead than any we leave behind. —C. S. Lewis

Heaven goes by favor; if we went by merit, you would stay out and your dog would go. —Mark Twain/Samuel L. Clemens (A distant relative of mine. My grandmother's maiden name was Clemons, a variant spelling, and she was from a town near the Mississippi River.)

Heaven is a prepared place for prepared people. —Dwight L. Moody

NOTES

Publisher's Preface

1. Mark Galli, "Incredible Journeys: What to Make of Visits to Heaven," *Christianity Today*, December 21, 2012, http://www.ctlibrary.com/ct/2012/december/incredible-journeys.html.

Chapter 4 From Heaven to Earth

1. Commonly called "Jaws of Life," this is a brand of tools trademarked by the Hurst Jaws of Life Company. The term refers to several types of piston-rod hydraulic tools known as cutters, spreaders, and rams that are used to pry trapped victims from crashed vehicles.

2. "What a Friend We Have in Jesus," words by Joseph Scriven, 1855.

Chapter 18 The *Why* Questions

1. Pim van Lommel, Ruud van Wees, Vincent Meyers, Ingrid Elffench, "Near-death Experience in Survivors of Cardiac Arrest: A Prospective Study in the Netherlands," *Lancet* 358, no. 9298 (December 15, 2001): 2039–45.

Stories of Encouragement

1. Dan Brannan, "Author Brings Comfort to Church Struck by Tragedy," *The Telegraph* (May 1, 2009), http://www.thetelegraph.com/news/piper-26313-church-winters.html.

My Favorite Bible Verses and Quotations

1. Donald Miller, *A Million Miles in a Thousand Years* (Thomas Nelson, 2009), 197.

Don Piper has been an ordained minister since 1985 and has served in several capacities on church staffs, including six years as a senior pastor. He and his wife, Eva, are residents of Pasadena, Texas, and are the parents of three grown children. Don has appeared on numerous Christian and secular television and radio programs and has been the subject of countless newspaper and magazine features. He has published four books and contributed to many others. Every week you will find him preaching and leading conferences and retreats all over the United States and abroad. Don can be contacted at donpiperministries@yahoo.com.

Cecil Murphey has written or cowritten more than one hundred books including *Gifted Hands: The Ben Carson Story*. Cecil can be contacted at www.cecilmurphey.com.

BASED ON THE INCREDIBLE TRUE STORY ...

90 MINUTES IN HEAVEN

STARRING HAYDEN CHRISTENSEN AND KATE BOSWORTH

HOPE LIVES

Pastor Don Piper died January 18, 1989 when a semi-tractor truck crushed his car. Declared dead by the first rescue workers to arrive on the scene, Don's body lay under a tarp for the next 90 minutes. Don's soul, meanwhile, was experiencing love, joy, and life like he'd never known before. Don was in heaven.

90 MINUTES IN HEAVEN brings to life the beloved book in a new feature-length film starring Hayden Christensen and Kate Bosworth, along with Michael W. Smith, Fred Thompson, Jason Kennedy, and Dwight Yoakam.

It's the movie that shares the eternal message that hope lives!

90MINUTESINHEAVENTHEMOVIE.COM

f 90MINUTESINHEAVENFILM **𝕏** @90MINUTESHEAVEN

© 2015 Giving Films, LLC. All Rights Reserved.

Connect with Don
at
Don Piper Ministries

www.DonPiperMinistries.com
www.90MinutesInHeaven.com

f Don Piper

- *Follow Don's speaking schedule*
- *Invite Don to speak to your group*
- *Subscribe to the newsletter*
- *Small group discussion guide available*

EXPERIENCE MARV BESTEMAN'S UNFORGETTABLE TRIP TO THE GATES OF HEAVEN AND BACK.

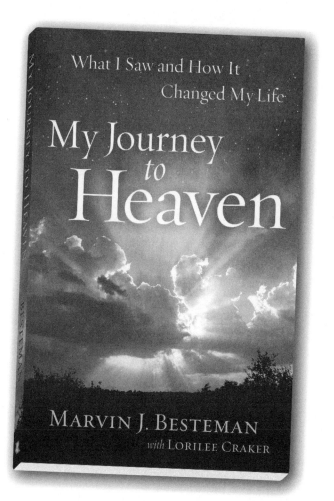

Revell

a division of Baker Publishing Group
www.RevellBooks.com

Available wherever books and ebooks are sold.

Through the eyes of a child, we see glimpses of heaven

"These stories will rock your world. I know I will never be the same again after reading *Touching Heaven*."

—**LEONARD SWEET**, bestselling author, professor at Drew University and George Fox University, and chief contributor to Sermons.com

Revell
a division of Baker Publishing Group
www.RevellBooks.com

Available wherever books and ebooks are sold.

TRUE STORIES OF HOPE AND PEACE AT THE END OF LIFE'S JOURNEY

Revell
a division of Baker Publishing Group
www.RevellBooks.com

Available Wherever Books Are Sold
Also Available in Ebook Format

Be the First to Hear about Other New Books from REVELL!

Sign up for announcements about new and upcoming titles at

RevellBooks.com/SignUp

Don't miss out on our great reads!

a division of Baker Publishing Group
www.RevellBooks.com